Also by Christa Kinde

The Threshold Series

The Blue Door (Book One)

The Hidden Deep (Book Two)

The Broken Window (Book Three)

THE BROKEN WINDOW

THRESHOLD SERIES

THE BROKEN WINDOW

BOOK THREE

CHRISTA KINDE

ZONDERKIDZ

The Broken Window

This title is also available as a Zondervan ebook.
Visit www.zondervan.com/ebooks.

Requests for information should be addressed to:

Zonderkidz, *5300 Patterson Ave SE, Grand Rapids, Michigan 49530*

ISBN: 978-0-310-72491-9

Published in association with KLO Publishing Service, LLC (*www.KLOPublishing.com*).

Cover design: Cindy Davis
Editor: Kim Childress
Interior design and composition: Greg Johnson/Textbook Perfect

Printed in the United States of America

---

13 14 15 16 17 18 /DCI/ 20 19 18 17 16 15 14 13 12 11 10 9 8 7 6 5 4 3 2 1

For all those who crave friendship—
May you find the one who needs yours.

TABLE OF CONTENTS

1

THE FIRST SNOW

In the small bedroom tucked under one of the dormers in the Pomeroys' farmhouse, a burst of silver light heralded the arrival of an angel. It was as if a door opened in the middle of the room, and when it closed, Abner stood on the braided rug. He absentmindedly poked the bridge of his nose, trying to adjust glasses he wasn't wearing at the moment. Long, silver hair swished as he turned and inspected the snug space. The ceiling sloped so dramatically that the top corner of the bedroom door was cut at an angle, and a wide seat stretched under a stained glass window, its pattern of multicolored diamonds shining faintly in the moonlight.

"So this is where you've been holed up," Abner said, cool gray eyes fixed upon Tamaes. The Guardian sat in the corner, arms folded stubbornly over his chest. "Jedrick said it might take heaven and earth to move you, so he sent me."

"This is where I am needed," protested Tamaes in a low voice.

Nodding at the girl asleep on her bed, the Caretaker said, "You cannot protect her from the inevitable."

The Guardian's gaze slid sideways. "She can hear my voice."

"Hearing and listening are two *very* different things, and there is *another* voice she must learn to heed." Crouching before Tamaes, Abner firmly said, "I'm sending you out to stretch your wings."

"And if I decline?"

"You won't, but if you *did*, I'd simply have the rest of the Hedge carry you off."

With a sigh, Tamaes begged for understanding. "She is my responsibility."

"While that's true, you're not alone," Abner reminded. "Taweel is on the roof, and Koji is down the hall. Even Omri would fly to her defense if the need were great."

"This is not the first time I have been asked to show more faith in my teammates."

"Then the lesson has yet to be learned." Standing, the silver-haired angel arranged himself on Prissie's windowseat. "I'll remain here until your return. I may not be a Guardian, but few are foolish enough to threaten a Caretaker."

"That is not true," Tamaes said, an ironic smile tugging at the long scar running down the side of his face. At Abner's quirked brow, he flatly added, "*No one* would dare."

Prissie leaned her forehead against a green diamond in the stained glass window so she could peer through a peach one.

Although a little better, she still had a fever, so the cold glass felt good against her flushed face. School was out for the day, and she was watching her brothers in the snow-filled yard below. Fat, sticky flakes drifted over their whole farm, blanketing everything under several inches of white stuff. This was the first big snow of the season, and it was perfect for packing.

Grandpa Pete was clearing the driveway with one of the tractors while the boys shoveled the walkways. Well, that's what they were *supposed* to be doing. Instead, they were goofing off, and Prissie had to admit, it looked like fun.

Neil's red Warriors stocking cap was pulled low over his blond hair as he threw snowballs as fast as he could make them. Since he played quarterback on their high school's football team, his aim was deadly. Tad retaliated by pitching whole shovelfuls of snow in his younger brother's direction.

Gently tracing the edges of a blue diamond, Prissie shifted so she could watch Beau through a soft yellow pane. Until her birthday in January, Prissie and Beau were the same age—fourteen. Her almost-twin was showing Koji how to roll a huge snowball, the kind you need for building snowmen. The two must have had big plans, because they called Neil over to help them push the monster boulder back across the lawn. Koji paused long enough in his play to look up at her window and wave one mittened hand. Even from a distance, Prissie could tell he was happy. She pressed her palm against her window, an answering smile creeping onto her lips.

Just then, the rumble of an engine and squeak of air brakes sounded from the direction of the road. The elementary school bus had arrived in the turnaround at the end of Orchard Lane. If Prissie leaned a little, she could just see her other two brothers chasing one another up the driveway. Zeke was already scooping handfuls of snow, eager to join Neil's battle. Jude trotted after him. Prissie knew that her youngest sibling would go to Tad first before checking on the chickens. But then the little boy suddenly wheeled and ran back the other way. Zeke also turned and charged after him. A moment later, another figure came into view. Milo Leggett waded toward the house, a package tucked under his arm, and two boys wrapped around his long legs.

At the sight of their mailman, Prissie's heart beat a little faster. Milo's blue eyes lifted to her bedroom window, and she jerked backward, hoping the stained glass hid her from view. Prissie's fondness for the Messenger had changed shape in recent months, but that didn't mean she wanted him to see her like this. "I must be a mess," she mumbled, pushing unhappily at honey-colored hair that probably looked as limp as she felt.

The boys crowded around the mailman, who gestured broadly while he talked. Before long, Milo had her brothers laughing, and Prissie was feeling more than a little left out. It wasn't fair that she was the only one still struggling to get better.

With a sigh, she glanced down at the notebook propped on her knees. December was almost here, so she was making her list and checking it twice. She wanted to give presents to several new people this year. Christmas was Prissie's favorite holiday, and she loved the decorations and the baking, the secrets and the presents. Grandpa Pete had begun humming snatches of Handel's *Messiah* while he worked, and Zeke was already laboring over a mile-long wish list. Prissie could hardly wait for the tree to go up in the family room or for the flood of holiday deliveries that would bring Milo to their door almost every afternoon.

At this time of the year, Prissie dearly missed Aunt Ida, who used to fill the house with carols from the piano in the corner of the family room. Her dad's younger sister had always been Prissie's best secret-keeper during Christmastime. Aunt Ida knew how to add bits of dough to gingerbread men so that they each had their own personality and how to cut apples so they looked like bunnies. Prissie could do these things for herself now, but it wasn't quite as much fun without her bubbly aunt.

Prissie stole another peek out the window in time to see Milo bend down to say something to Koji, who nodded seriously and hurried to the door. Glancing up over his shoulder, the mailman caught her watching and winked. Then, her brothers dragged him over to inspect their giant snowball, which Zeke promptly scaled.

By the time Koji opened her bedroom door, Prissie had worked up a good sulk. "You're not supposed to come in here without permission," she grumbled at her closest friend.

He studied her face and politely inquired, "Should I leave?"

"No," she said grudgingly, pulling up her quilt to hide her flaming cheeks. She was as tired of being alone as she was of being sick.

Koji stepped into the room and padded over on stocking feet. "There are messages for you!" he announced, clearly pleased to be entrusted with their delivery.

The postcard was from Aunt Ida, and Prissie smiled as she skimmed its brief note. "She and Uncle Lo are in Africa now," she said. "And she hopes we have snow."

"We do," he answered seriously.

"Obviously."

"There is *another* message," Koji said.

Prissie eyed his empty hands. "From whom?"

"Milo."

"Really?" she murmured, stealing another glance outside. Koji climbed onto the opposite end of the window seat and let one foot swing while he watched the activity in the yard below. When he took the time to scan the sky as well, she asked, "Is everything all right?"

"There is nothing to fear," Koji replied. Then he relayed the Messenger's request. "If you would not mind, Milo will come for you in dreams tonight. Jedrick has called a meeting."

Prissie took the time to comb and braid her hair, but she didn't go downstairs when the dinner bell rang. Her mom came to check on her, pressing a cool hand to her daughter's forehead. "You could join us," she invited. "If you're up to it?"

"Is Milo staying for supper?" Prissie asked suspiciously.

"Yes."

"I don't want to get him sick."

"Are you sure?"

Prissie's chin lifted stubbornly. "Yes."

"Get some rest, then," Mrs. Pomeroy encouraged. "My folks are going along to the rehearsal tonight, so once the house is quiet, I'll bring up a tray. Sound good?"

"I guess," Prissie sighed. "Thanks, Momma."

Her maternal grandparents had been visiting since just before Thanksgiving. Grandpa Carl and Grammie Esme's RV was parked next to the apple barn, but they were staying in the spare room at Grandpa Pete and Grandma Nell's house.

Grandpa Carl said they would stick around until after the annual production of Handel's *Messiah,* then they would follow the snowbirds south for the winter.

The Christmas concert was only a couple weeks away, and excitement was building. This year, the decision had been made to mix things up a bit by doing a modern twist on the classic. Grandpa Pete, who'd been singing with the bass section for forty years, had been suspicious about the introduction of drums and electric guitars to the orchestra, but it cheered him immensely that two of his grandsons had joined the choir this year.

Prissie was actually just as excited about the upcoming concert, mostly because Milo was taking part for the first time. He'd been coaxed into it by his good friend Baird, another angel-in-disguise who led worship at a church down in Harper.

At some point, Prissie must have drifted off because she was roused from a fitful doze by the rattle of dishes and shuffle of feet. Lifting her head from her pillow, she squinted into the light from the hallway while Koji carefully maneuvered through the door with a tray of food. "Why didn't you go to rehearsal?" she asked in surprise.

"Your mother says this goes on your lap," the boy announced, putting off his answer. "Sit up, please."

Prissie reached across to flick on her bedside lamp, then did as she was bidden. Koji set the tray before her and sat down at the foot of the bed. "This is the first time I have prepared food for someone. Please, eat it."

"You cooked?"

Koji's happiness came through loud and clear. "I did!"

"Did you have fun?"

"Your mother was very encouraging," he replied seriously. "I hope it will be satisfying."

Prissie dutifully picked up her fork and tasted the scrambled eggs, then took a bite of cinnamon toast. "It's good," she assured with a small smile. "Thank you."

He nodded, then addressed her initial question. "I remained behind because you are here."

"You shouldn't have to miss out just because I'm sick," Prissie said. "Rehearsals are one of the only times you get to see Harken, Baird, and Kester!"

Dark eyes gazed steadily into hers, as if he was trying to figure out what she *meant* by what she said. Finally, Koji asked, "Have you forgotten your promise?"

Nibbling at her toast, Prissie replied, "No, of course I remember." Back in October, the young angel had been given permission to secure a promise from her. She'd given her word not to wander off by herself. It was almost as if the young Observer was trying to be her second guardian angel. "I've kept my promise too!"

"You have," he agreed. "In a covenant of this nature, we *both* have a promise to keep."

That hadn't occurred to her. "So when I promised to stay with you, you were also promising to stay with me?"

"Indeed."

Prissie poked at her dinner and murmured, "I'm sorry."

"Why?"

"Because you're stuck with me, I guess."

Koji blinked. "This is where I want to be."

"But what if you wanted to do something else?"

He calmly replied, "There is nothing else I wish to do."

"But if you *did*!"

"Do you still not understand?" he asked, the hint of a smile twitching at the corner of his lips.

"I guess not," she grumbled, but at the same time, she was very glad. It was completely like Koji to take a promise seriously. He'd been a faithful friend from the very beginning, a fact that warmed her heart. "But that's okay, right?"

With a smile that lived up to the description *angelic*, Koji repeated, "Indeed."

"It is late," Koji whispered. The rest of the household was completely still when he tiptoed back to her room. "You need to sleep."

"I slept all day," Prissie complained. "I'm not tired."

With a soft hum, he knelt beside her bed, and his fingers brushed across the back of her hand. "What does sickness feel like?"

"Bad."

"I can see that you are uncomfortable." He gently fitted his hand into hers and asked, "What else?"

Prissie sighed, but at least Koji's curiosity provided a distraction. Staring up at the ceiling, she replied, "When you're sick, it's like everything goes wrong. I felt weak, dizzy, achy. One minute, I was too hot, and the next, I was shivering. Now, I just feel *blah*."

"What does *blah* mean?" he asked curiously.

"Bored, restless, and very tired of being sick," she replied moodily.

"Tired, but not sleepy," he mused aloud. "You long for rest and cannot find it."

"Yes. And it doesn't help knowing that everyone's waiting for me to fall asleep."

"Time is of no consequence." Koji tipped his head to one side and said, "I am permitted to offer a suggestion."

"Permitted?" she echoed, rolling onto her side to face him. It still struck her as strange that he sometimes received instructions directly from heaven ... or from his teammates.

Koji nodded. "Harken says that Marcus says that you are forgetting something he already told you."

Prissie blinked at the relayed message, then frowned. Marcus might be an angel, but he annoyed her more often than not. "I have no idea what he means."

The young Observer's eyes shifted out of focus, and then he nodded to himself. With a small smile, he said, "Harken says that Marcus says to stop dawdling and ask for what you need."

"And what's that?" she groused.

Koji gave her hand a squeeze. "I do not need sleep, so I will keep you company."

Oh. With a longsuffering sigh, she closed her eyes and tried to relax. Thoughts wandered, but she rebelled against taking advice from Marcus. Still, it would be Milo who came for her, and that was something she'd been looking forward to since that afternoon. With a much smaller sigh, she offered an awkward little prayer, asking for the sleep she needed in order to join the dream where her angelic friends waited.

Prissie had sort of expected the dream to begin as her last one had, with starlight and candlelight, but nothing was the same. Sounds came first, a strange sort of clinking, like melting ice cubes in a glass of water, and then Milo's voice reached her. "Miss Priscilla? Open your eyes, please."

She obeyed, and immediately squinted. She was seated on the ground, but blue surrounded her, bright as the sky on a sunny day. Translucent layers of luminescent color draped around the two of them, creating a sheltering cocoon.

Milo smiled at her in his same old way, though he no longer would have passed as their small town's mailman. His ash blond hair tumbled in a riot of curls that reached well past his shoulders, and he was dressed in raiment. The beige cloth glowed with a life of its own. Glancing down, Prissie saw that she, too, wore new clothes, a simple dress as white as new snow. Turning wondering eyes on the Messenger, whose hands were folded together in a relaxed manner, she murmured, "It's different!"

"What is?"

"This isn't anything like when Koji came for me," she explained, a tinge of accusation in her tone.

"I should hope not!" he exclaimed, eyes sparkling with good humor. "That was Koji's very first attempt to reach out to someone in dreams. While he managed very well with Harken's assistance, I'm a full-fledged Messenger. This is what I *do*!"

Again, there was a distant tinkle of sound, and her attention was drawn to the bright blue folds that hemmed them in. "This is beautiful," she quietly confided.

"Thank you," he replied just as softly.

"Where are we?"

"In the garden behind the blue door."

"I don't remember anything like this there," she murmured, tentatively reaching out to touch the melodic light. He watched her exploration without comment, which Prissie took as permission to continue. Color slipped over her fingers like nothing she'd ever encountered—softer than silk, lighter than air. It tickled across her skin like a breeze, and brought a smile to her face. Finally, she asked, "What is all this?"

Milo's eyebrows lifted slightly. "My wings."

Snatching her hand back, she murmured, "Oooh! Excuse me!"

"It's all right, Miss Priscilla. Ready to see the others?"

"Yes, please."

Nodding once, the Messenger gave his wings a gentle shake, then lifted them away, slowly revealing a familiar forest glade. Yahavim zipped around like golden fireflies, but for once, she ignored the little manna-makers. Prissie had been hoping to see Milo's wings since the first moment she realized he had them, and she stared in frank admiration. Propping his chin on his hand, he wafted them playfully and asked, "Satisfied?"

Prissie toyed with the end of her braid and mumbled an indistinct affirmative. Glancing around, she spied Tamaes leaning against a nearby tree, a faint smile on his face. Her guardian angel was garbed as usual in armor-covered raiment, and the hilt of a sword showed over his shoulder. Sleek auburn hair partially hid the scar that ran along one side of his face, and for once, his wings weren't on full display. Instead, a vivid pattern of overlapping rings in shades of orange decorated his arms.

When Tamaes caught her eye, he strode forward to offer one large, tanned hand, helping her to her feet. "Hello, Prissie," he greeted, searching her face with ill-concealed concern.

"I'm fine," she blurted.

He shook his head. "You are ill."

"I'm mostly better," she argued, vaguely embarrassed to have worried him. "I'll be better soon."

"May it be so," Tamaes said, and his gaze drifted off to one side. "Hello, Koji."

She turned in surprise to find her friend hanging back, simply observing. Milo chuckled and asked, "Is Jedrick expecting you as well?"

Koji self-consciously tucked his loose hair behind an ear that now came to a distinct point. "I was not invited, but I need to stay with Prissie."

"Oh, sure," interjected a familiar voice. "Where would she be without her conscience?"

Prissie turned to see Marcus strolling toward them through the trees beside Jedrick. It was slightly disorienting to see a classmate wearing armor and heavy boots with oddly woven straps, but Marcus looked right at home in his raiment.

"Her *conscience*?" inquired the Flight captain.

"It is a nickname," Koji offered seriously.

From what Prissie could tell, the warrior types in Jedrick's Flight wore sleeveless tunics. The Protector towered imposingly over the rest of them, all broad shoulders and bulging muscles. When he folded strong arms over his chest, she noticed that his fair skin was laced by an intricate pattern of green whorls. In contrast, Marcus's wings had settled into jagged markings that zigzagged in hues of cream and yellow over his warm brown skin.

Standing as tall as he could beside his mentor, Marcus also crossed his arms and smirked infuriatingly at Prissie. "Took you long enough, kiddo!" Before she could work up some indignation, Jedrick rumpled Marcus's two-tone hair, causing the younger angel to duck his head and protest, "I was only saying *hi*!" The apprentice Protector might have been able to carry off a tough guy aura at school, but next to the other warriors in his Flight, he was pretty puny.

Prissie's soft giggle put an end to the jostling, and Jedrick suggested, "Shall we begin?"

She asked, "Are we the only ones here?"

The captain explained, "These four spend the most time with you." That made sense, and when she nodded, Jedrick continued. "I cannot say if you have come to know us because you are in danger, or if you are in danger because you have come to know us. Either way, the threat is real, for Adin seems to have singled you out."

"And he's a demon?"

"He has set himself against God," Jedrick confirmed.

Prissie didn't *exactly* doubt them. Adin had been polite, handsome, and stylish ... but sometimes he said or did things that made her uneasy. Frowning in concentration, she asked Jedrick, "How can you tell? I thought demons were horrible monsters."

Marcus snorted, and with a dramatic flash of light, he unfurled his wings, spreading them wide. Getting right in her face, he made certain she was staring into his eyes, which were an impossible shade of gold. "Look at me, Prissie," he demanded in exasperation. "Is *this* how I show up to school?"

"Obviously not."

"You already know the Faithful can hide their true nature in order to fit in! It's no different for the Fallen!"

"Fine. But if he's an enemy, how do you know his name? Is he on some kind of Most Wanted list?"

For several moments, an awkward silence filled the glade. Jedrick sighed and nodded at Tamaes, who took a half-step forward. "Adin and I were once close," her Guardian said dully. "He was like a brother to me when I was newly formed."

"What happened?" Prissie asked, aghast.

With a small shrug, Tamaes replied, "He Fell."

"That's all?"

Koji tapped her hand and solemnly answered, "That is *everything.*"

Jedrick cleared his throat and fixed Prissie with a stern gaze. "The members of my Flight stand ready to back up Tamaes in his service to God. Come what may, we are with you."

Then Milo stepped forward. "I have a message for you, Miss Priscilla."

"An official one?" she asked warily.

"Yep. And it's threefold."

"Oh," she managed, her heart already racing.

Holding up a finger, Milo said, "Trust."

Prissie had expected more than one word, so it took her a moment to react. "Isn't that the same message Harken gave me before?"

Raising a second finger, Milo said, "Listen."

Even more stymied, she asked, "To *what*?"

The Messenger replied, "At the moment, to *me*." A third finger joined the others, and Milo concluded, "Remember."

Truly frustrated now, Prissie begged, "Remember *what*?"

Marcus grumbled something about a complete lack of awe where divine messages were concerned, but Milo only chuckled. "I don't know, Miss Priscilla. However, I can say with absolute certainty that whatever it is, it must be important."

2

THE OPEN HOUSE

The hum was barely there, a whisper of sound. Ephron wasn't ashamed to be heard, nor did he fear the consequences should his captors overhear his feeble notes. Only weakness kept him from raising his voice any higher.

Although the captive angel's tattered raiment shed dirt, his pale skin was powdered by dust, darkened by bruises, and traced by cuts, blood, and tears. The unforgiving stone of the pit's floor was strewn with hanks of flaxen hair, evidence of Murque's latest game. What remained of the Observer's former glory hung raggedly around his shoulders. He leaned his head back against the rough wall and longed for heaven's brightness, the familiar chorus of evensong with friends, and the One whom he loved above all others.

Heart aching, voice cracking, the lonely angel bravely continued to sing of light in the midst of an endless night. Even if it was his last breath, Ephron would spend it in worship.

Late the following afternoon, loneliness drove Prissie from the confines of her bedroom to the kitchen table. She was much improved today, so Momma had decreed her fit for school tomorrow. Tad and Koji kept her company, both engrossed in their own studies. Prissie glanced up from her make-up homework as Neil tromped into the kitchen, his arms laden with bags, talking to Grandpa Carl.

"Nope. Coach Hobbes bumped me up to the varsity team, but I didn't really get a lot of time on the field."

"Were you disappointed?" his grandfather asked, coming in behind him and sliding a box onto the counter.

"I *was* a little," Neil said. "But Tim's graduating. I knew if I hung in there, I'd be the starting quarterback *next* year. Gramps told me to look smart and learn all I could." Shrugging nonchalantly, he added, "It's cool."

Beau ambled into the room, peering curiously into the various bags, probably looking for something to munch. "Don't spoil dinner," Prissie warned.

Grandpa Carl nudged Neil and stage whispered, "Best not mention those burgers we demolished."

"What?" Prissie exclaimed.

"Unfair!" agreed Beau.

"Kidding," said Neil, rolling his eyes at their grandfather. Then he wrapped an arm around Beau's shoulders. "O, brother of mine! Lend me your geek factor for a while?"

"What for?"

Neil tapped the box on the counter. "*This* is gonna be awesome. Probably. Assuming you can figure out how it works … ?"

Beau inspected the label. "A police scanner?"

"Dad said it was okay, so we picked it up," Neil explained. "Derrick told me that a lot of the other volunteer firemen have them."

"I'll help," Beau agreed. "Where do you want to set it up?"

"My room!"

As Prissie's two brothers thumped up the back stairs, Grandpa Carl sidled over to her. "How are you feeling, fussbudget?"

"Better today."

"Glad to hear it!" he cheerfully replied before taking a covert survey of the room. Then from the depths of his jacket pocket, he withdrew a small, white paper sack, which he slid across the kitchen table. "A little something to keep up your strength."

The bag was filled with penny candy, and she smiled. "Thanks, Grandpa!"

He winked. "Don't spoil your appetite."

After classes a couple days later, Mr. Pomeroy swung by school in the van to pick up a few helping hands for work at the bakery. Koji and Prissie piled in while her father looked over the crowd of milling students. "Where's Ransom?"

"I wouldn't know," she replied. "I'm *not* his keeper."

"There he is," Koji said, pointing confidently. "Marcus is with him."

Prissie sat a little straighter as both teens ambled over to the driver's side to talk to her father. To her astonishment, Ransom introduced Marcus, and to her chagrin, both boys circled around to get inside. As they slid into the row behind hers, she stared blankly at the apprentice Protector. "What are *you* doing here?"

"Bumming a ride," Marcus replied, casually draping his arms along the back of his seat.

Something occurred to her, and she turned to Koji and muttered, "*Please* tell me Jennifer didn't see him get into our van."

Koji didn't miss much. "She is there. With Elise and Margery."

Following his gaze, Prissie winced at the sight of Jennifer Ruiz's sulky scowl. Ever since Marcus rescued Prissie from the tunnels near the Deep a couple months ago, Jennifer had been convinced Prissie was trying to steal him from her. The accusation was ridiculous on so many levels, but it also hurt.

As the van pulled out onto the highway, Ransom tapped her shoulder. "He just needed a ride into town, Miss Priss." He gave her a searching look. "Marcus *isn't* a bad guy."

Although she bristled at his cautionary tone, she replied honestly. "I know."

He seemed stunned by her frank acceptance, and Marcus hid his smile by staring out the window at passing scenery. "Never woulda saw that one coming, but I won't complain." Shaking his head, Ransom remarked, "You're a hard one to figure, Miss Priss."

With a toss of braids, she faced the front and pretended neither of them was there. Honestly! It wasn't as if she'd ever be rude in front of her father, and even if she could never explain *why,* she trusted Marcus. How could she not? Oh, she wished he'd act a little more angelic, and maybe fix his ridiculous hair. But he was a Protector. And that changed things.

Prissie frowned to herself as she thought back to the few

times she'd seen Marcus when he wasn't masquerading as a human. His eye color had gone from brown to gold, but his hair hadn't changed at all. If that was the case, didn't that mean that bi-colored hair was exactly what God intended for him? She was beginning to get the idea that the Creator was quite *creative* in His tastes. Green hair? Purple eyes? Rainbow-hued wings? She *tsk*-ed softly to herself, then immediately felt irreverent.

Prissie wanted to ask about it all, but she certainly wasn't going to turn to Marcus. Making a mental note to bring it up later to Koji, she glanced his way. The Observer's eyes were on her face, and his countenance seemed brighter than usual. "What?" she whispered.

Leaning close so as not to be overheard, he replied, "When your thoughts turn toward God, it pleases Him."

Her eyes widened. "Are you sure you can't read minds?"

"Not at all," he assured.

"Then, how ... ?"

Koji gave her question some thought, then quietly answered, "I believe I am attuned to worship, and your spirit and His Spirit were in harmony."

Prissie was certain she'd never cease to be amazed by the things Koji shared.

Once they reached Loafing Around, Marcus tossed them a wave and wandered off by himself. Mr. Pomeroy herded the rest of them inside and sent them to the sinks to wash up. "Aprons all around!" he decreed before going to inspect the progress of his other assistants.

The bakery was getting ready for its annual Christmas

open house, which was always planned for the first Saturday in December. It was the day Prissie's dad started adding holiday treats to the bakery case and accepting pre-orders for parties. His breads and Auntie Lou's pies were very popular, but the real draw during the festive kick-off party was their cookies.

Sugar cookies in all shapes and sizes were decorated with fussy icing, sparkling sugars, and colorful sprinkles. They were a Pomeroy tradition that Jayce shared with all his customers, with a little help from his family and friends. Grandma Nell and Grammie Esme were already in the bakery's big kitchen, chatting with Auntie Lou as they patiently piped icing onto cookies shaped like bells, stars, trees, and snowflakes. Pearl had traded her knitting needles for a pair of tweezers and was patiently adding details to a snowman from a pile of candy confetti. Even Uncle Lou was getting into the spirit of things, adding a glossy coating of sanding sugar to an apple-shaped cookie.

"Whoa!" Ransom exclaimed, his eyes lighting up. "I *love* my job!"

"Oooh, who's this nice, young man?" Grammie Esme asked, peering at him over the red frames of her reading glasses.

Mr. Pomeroy quickly made introductions while Ransom tied his apron, then the teen claimed the chair next to Pearl's and asked, "What can I do?"

"Whatever you like, dear," Auntie Lou invited, waving at the array of icings. "You too, Koji."

The Observer readily joined the group, though he seemed content to look and not touch.

Prissie wasn't thrilled with the idea of leaving Ransom in

the same room with both her grandmothers. The potential for disaster was enormous, and she really wished Beau was there to help stem the tide of tales. At the same time, she was pleased and proud to have been singled out as her father's helper for the afternoon. Jayce always built an elaborate gingerbread house in the bakery's front window, assembling it right there, where everyone could watch him work.

"Ready to do some roofing?" he asked.

For nearly an hour, they worked in tandem, patiently overlapping rounds of dark chocolate until the whole roof was neatly scalloped. After that, he set Prissie to work braiding licorice whips while he used pillow candy to cobble a sidewalk. Time passed pleasantly, smelling of spice and peppermint and interspersed with her dad's questions about this and that.

Finally, he stood back. "That'll do for today, I think. I can add the finishing touches tomorrow morning."

"It looks great," Prissie declared.

"Anything missing?"

"How about a mailbox?"

"Good idea!" he exclaimed, rummaging through his containers of candy for a large gumdrop, which he began to knead. "Why don't you check on progress in the back? We'll need to wrap up soon, or your mother will think I've forgotten the way home."

Prissie was still smiling over the nonsensical remark when she pushed through the swinging door into the kitchen. Ransom glanced up, and his eyebrows did their funny little quirk thing; however, he went right back to his decorating duties without comment. She noticed that he handled a piping bag like a pro ... unlike Koji. The tabletop around his workspace was liberally daubed with dribbles of icing, and there was an explosion of sprinkles on both floor and table. To his credit, his cookies looked all right, so she only asked, "Having fun?"

"Indeed." The Observer's face was a picture of concentration as he added a pinch of purple jimmies to a purple-frosted star. Eyeing his handiwork, Prissie realized that he was once more reaching for stars. They were the only shape he'd decorated, and there were so many colors, the collection resembled a kaleidoscope.

"It's almost dinnertime," Prissie announced.

"So it is," Auntie Lou murmured with a glance at her watch.

Grandma Nell capped the jars of colored sugar closest to her. "I'll just give your mom a call."

Koji quickly offered to sweep, and Prissie lent a hand with putting on the remaining caps and lids. As she moved along the table, she cast a critical glance over the cookies closest to Ransom. "Which ones did you do?" she asked curiously.

Setting aside the icing, he gestured broadly. "Most of these are mine. Pearl was putting hers on the counter behind you."

There was nothing to criticize ... except maybe that all the reindeer sported pink noses. But since it was sort of cute that way, she shrugged it off. "They look really good," she admitted.

"You sound surprised."

"Maybe I am," she retorted. "None of my brothers take the time to do cookies right. All they care about is eating them."

Ransom grinned. "You're my witness, Koji. Miss Priss just said I did something *right*!"

Mr. Pomeroy strolled through the door at that moment.

"You can come in and help him when he does the next batch, Princess."

"No, thank you." The last thing she wanted to do was spend more time with Ransom outside of school. "I have a lot more people on my list this year, so I need extra time to shop."

Her father favored her with a long look. "In that case, I suggest you make room in your schedule for the icing, and maybe some of the baking as well. You could use the extra income, and I could use an extra pair of hands."

"You'll pay me?"

"I have room in my budget for some holiday help," he agreed.

"Thanks, Dad!" She paused, thinking. "Would it be okay if Koji helps too?"

Smiling warmly at the young angel who'd been living under his roof, Mr. Pomeroy said, "Sure, sure. As your mother says, the more the merrier."

Prissie was happy to be lending a hand during the open house, especially since Ransom *wasn't* there for once. Humming along to the Christmas carols on the radio Pearl kept behind the counter, she wiped tables and made sure the bread racks were stocked. Saturday mornings were mostly filled with regulars, so Jayce and Auntie Lou visited with friends and neighbors while they did a brisk business in Loafing Around's famous potato rolls.

Glancing around the bakery's small dining area, Prissie couldn't shake the feeling that she'd forgotten something. Running through her mental checklist of duties, she couldn't figure out what, but every time there was a lull in the activity, the nagging feeling resurfaced. She was still puzzling when the bell over the door jangled, letting in a gust of cold air and another customer. Turning with a ready smile, Prissie gasped, "Padgett! What brings you here?"

"I was in the neighborhood," he replied. Padgett Prentice worked as a ranger at Sunderland State Park, north and east of town and nearly adjacent to the Pomeroys' farm. With his high cheekbones and black braid, he looked Native American, but he was actually another member of Jedrick's Flight. "This is my first time visiting your family's bakery."

Prissie couldn't think why the Caretaker might suddenly decide to drop in and anxiously asked, "Is anything wrong?"

He studied her face. "Does something seem to be wrong?"

That gave her pause. Something *had* been bothering her all day, and she couldn't put her finger on it. "Maybe," she admitted in a low voice. "I don't know *what*, and I don't know *why* ... but I have a funny feeling. It's hard to explain."

Padgett nodded patiently. "There are times when feelings are nothing more than that."

Prissie frowned. "So it's nothing?"

"I didn't say that," he gently countered. "However, letting emotions dictate your decisions can be as unwise as letting appearances influence your opinions."

She got the idea he'd said something very wise, but with no idea how to respond, Prissie asked, "Are you here to see Koji? He's in the back."

"I'd be pleased to see him, but I was not Sent for any specific purpose," he replied. "I'm here with my boss."

"Abner's here too?"

Padgett turned to the big front window. Sure enough,

Abner Ochs stood outside, his hands clasped behind his back as he bent low to scrutinize every lovingly laid detail on her father's gingerbread house. Lifting a finger, the apprentice signaled to his mentor. Abner entered and casually glanced around. "Coffee, I think."

"Yes, sir," Padgett replied. With a polite nod to Prissie, he took his place in the short line at the front counter.

Left alone with the balding park ranger, she said, "Good morning, Abner."

He gazed over the rims of his glasses. "Prissie Pomeroy," he mused aloud. "You seem better."

"You knew I was sick?"

"I did," he acknowledged. "If Tamaes were able to fend off illness with that blade of his, it would not have visited you."

"Oh, I suppose so. Say ... would you like to sit down?"

"If you'll join us."

"I'm sure that'd be fine." She followed him to one of the small tables.

Padgett brought two cups of coffee. He added cream and sugar to Abner's before passing it along, then sipped his black. Searching for something to say, Prissie began, "I was wondering about the time when I was lost in the caves. Afterward, Padgett ministered to me, and I felt better."

Abner's gaze swung to his apprentice. "Did you?"

"Yes, sir."

"Very thoughtful. The girl had a long day."

"Yes, sir," his apprentice agreed.

With an aggrieved look, Abner protested, "You don't have to call me *sir*, Mr. Prentice. We're not on duty at the moment."

Padgett only took another sip of his coffee. "You have a question, Prissie?

"I was just curious," she said. "You're able to minister to people. Could you have gotten rid of my fever?"

Abner inclined his head. "That's certainly within my realm of experience; however, such things aren't done according to my will."

"So you *could*, but you don't unless God tells you to?"

"I can do no more or less than what I am bidden."

Padgett quietly pointed out, "You already told her that, sir."

"Did I?"

"Yes, I remember," Prissie murmured. "I suppose I just didn't understand what you meant the first time."

With a small smile, Abner said, "Then you have benefited from the repetition. Many do."

The bell over the door jangled again, and Padgett remarked, "We should be getting back, sir."

Prissie glanced at the kitchen door, surprised that Koji hadn't put in an appearance yet. He had to know his teammates were here. "Will I see you again soon?" she asked, oddly reluctant to let them go.

"I don't have any way of knowing," Abner replied candidly. "But if I were to guess, I'd say yes. Our paths are likely to cross again soon. If not in winter, then certainly in spring."

"Oh? Why then?"

Standing, Padgett explained, "Your class is one of those scheduled to visit the park in April."

"Which part?" Prissie asked curiously.

"The orienteering trails."

"Again?" With a shake of her head, she waved a hand. "I've been on those trails three or four times before!"

Abner's gaze was keen as he replied, "As you have already acknowledged, there is often a benefit to repetition."

3

THE UGLY WHISPERS

"She's utterly clueless," Marcus grumbled. "And childish."

Harken's deep chuckle rolled through the empty shop. "The faith of a child is precious in the sight of God."

The Protector shook his head incredulously. "This one has the faith of Thomas."

With a widening smile, the Messenger countered, "Then let her see, let her touch, and let her faith be strengthened."

Prissie knew she must be dreaming, for she often dreamed of the hayloft in the barn. It was a recurring nightmare grounded in a frightening fall during her early childhood. Her fear of heights lingered, and she automatically checked to see how close to the edge she was standing. But several things had changed from the usual pattern. For one, it was wintertime, although she wasn't cold, even with bare feet.

Also, it was nighttime. This dream had always taken place on a spring day, with sunlight streaming through cracks and between rafters. Turning to check the window near the peak of the roof, Prissie spied another major difference. She wasn't alone.

Padgett's raiment shone softly in the darkness as he worked his way across bales of straw on his hands and knees. He was barefoot too, and his long, black hair dragged on the ground as he shuffled along. For the life of her, Prissie couldn't figure out what he was doing, but the longer she watched, the more frightened she grew. His expression was solemn as he reached out to cup something that wasn't there, then pressed his hands firmly in midair. When he murmured something softly to no one, she finally whispered, "Padgett?"

"Prissie," he answered, sparing her a glance. "What brings you here?"

She blinked in confusion and dared to speak a little louder. "Shouldn't I be asking *you* that? This is *our* barn."

"I know, and I'm grateful for the haven it's become," he calmly replied. Shifting further along the row of bales, he distractedly asked, "How much can you see?"

"Only you. What are you doing?"

"Ministering to those in need."

So that was it. Someone else *was* here, someone she couldn't see. If that person needed a Caretaker's attention, it could only mean one thing. "Someone's hurt?"

"Yes."

Hugging herself, she squinted hard into the dimness, but it was no use. "Why can't I see what's happening?" she complained.

He turned inquiringly. "Do you wish to see?"

"I ... I think so."

Padgett nodded once. "Then open your eyes."

Suddenly, Prissie was surrounded by angels, and the combined light of their raiment banished the shadows. Unfurled wings lent splashes of color, but most of the wounded warriors bore distinctive tattoos on their arms and shoulders. Low groans, muffled voices, the scrape of boots, and the metallic *clank* of weapons filled the loft. The angels leaned against the walls or sat on the straw, but many were simply strewn across the floor.

With a soft noise of dismay, Prissie cautiously approached the nearest, appalled by the nasty wound showing just above his breastplate. As she knelt by his side, she realized that while he was bleeding, the blood wasn't red, and the gash glowed, as if angels were even brighter inside than out. That hardly mattered, though, for the angel's face was creased by pain. "Wh-what can I do?" she stammered. "Neil knows about first aid, but he's asleep. Maybe it would be better if he was here? Or Koji! I know *he* would help, if you asked him to come."

Padgett crouched beside her and turned her face so she could only see him. "Don't be afraid," he soothed. "I'll tend to them. That's why I was Sent here."

"Please?" she asked, teary-eyed in her dismay. "There are so many of them, and only one you!"

He cupped her cheek and almost-smiled. "When the Spirit compels, it is the same as Sending. God accepts your offering, child of compassion." He placed a roll of bandages in her hand. "Stay close."

The gauzy material Padgett used to bind wounds reminded Prissie of raiment, for it seemed to be woven from threads of light. As he worked, she peered in fascination at each of his patients, admiring the endless variety in coloration and trying to memorize each face. By the stitching along their collars, she gathered that most of the warriors were cherubim. Just like Jedrick, they were big, powerful angels with fierce countenances and stern expressions. No one seemed inclined to converse with her, but without fail, those who met her gaze greeted her with a soft, "Fear not." Their reassurances were touching, and before they were half done, Prissie's heart brimmed with an odd mix of awe and gratitude.

Just then, a tall angel with turquoise wings trod heavily across the wooden floor, half carrying an injured comrade. This Protector did a double-take when he noticed Prissie. "What is the meaning of this, Caretaker?"

"She is dreaming."

Helping his friend to the floor, the archer studied her face. "Will she remember?"

"I don't think so."

Prissie's gaze snapped to Padgett's face. "I'll forget all this?"

"Do you often remember your dreams?" he inquired.

"Only bits and pieces," she slowly admitted. "But this isn't a *dream* dream. This is really happening, isn't it?"

"Yes, Prissie," Padgett assured. "This is real."

"What if I don't *want* to forget?" she whispered, giving the inquisitive Protector a pleading look.

With a shake of his head that sent his long, wheat-colored ponytail swaying, the tall angel answered, "Such things are in the hands of God." Standing, he straightened the quiver of arrows strapped to his back. "I must rejoin my Flight."

"I'll tend to your teammate," Padgett promised.

The other angel nodded curtly and turned to go, but he paused to address Prissie. "Even if this memory fades, do not fear," he solemnly urged. "We shall remain. Indeed, we have always been nearby." Then, to her utter astonishment, he strode through an archway cut into the side of the barn, spread his wings, and took to the sky.

Pointing to the opening, Prissie exclaimed, "There's a *hole*?"

Padgett didn't even look up. "I opened a way, and I will close it when my task is complete."

She didn't want to get too close to the edge, but Prissie sidled a little closer so she could look through, and what she saw boggled her mind. The skies were filled with varicolored stars and the brilliant flash of angels' wings. It might have been beautiful if it hadn't been a battle.

The ranks of heavenly hosts clashed noisily with an enemy that was hard to make out in the darkness, but their shadowy forms were the stuff of nightmares. Broken wings creaked, foul voices bayed, and weapons slashed brutally. Prissie gripped the wall's edge and whimpered.

An angel standing guard at the entrance glanced her way, and when his silver eyes met her gaze, they widened. He quickly placed himself between her and the scenes of violence, dropping to one knee and lifting iridescent white wings to block her view of the battle beyond. "Hello, Prissie," he said, his deep voice gentle.

"You know me?"

"I do," he confirmed. "Do not be afraid, little daughter."

In complete contrast with his eyes and wings, the enormous angel's skin was black as jet. His hair stood out in a series of corkscrews around his head, and the hilts of two swords showed above his broad shoulders. Even though he had lowered himself to speak with her, he was nearly as tall as she, yet she wasn't frightened. He almost seemed ... familiar. Catching sight of the stitching on the edge of his collar, Prissie asked, "You're a Guardian? Does that mean you know Tamaes and Taweel?"

A slow smile spread across the angel's face. "We serve together in the Hedge."

"Hedge?"

"A gathering of Guardians," he explained. "We are hadarim, a hedge of protection set in place by God."

"Does that mean ... ?"

Padgett called to her then, and the silver-eyed warrior sighed. "That answer will come in the fullness of time. Go on, now."

She quickly returned to the Caretaker's side, and time seemed to stretch; perhaps it stood still. All through the night, she watched the comings and goings of supernatural strangers. These were the Faithful. Heaven was their home, the Lord was their love, and her protection was part of their duty. A few others paused to greet her and allay her fears, and the more she met, the more she cared. She wanted to do something, and a growing sense of urgency built in her heart. But what *could* she do? Feeling increasingly helpless, Prissie asked, "Is it always like this?"

"No." Padgett pushed his hair behind one pointed ear, inadvertently leaving a bright smudge of blood across his cheek. Shaking his head, he repeated, "No, it's not. The enemy has been gathering strength, and they attack with greater numbers each time they rise up."

"Why?"

"Why what?" he patiently inquired.

"Why are they attacking *here*?" she clarified.

"I cannot say for certain," the Caretaker replied as he brushed the hair out of the eyes of a suffering Protector. "This place has seen unrest for quite some time."

"Because of the Deep?"

"Perhaps. However, it's fair to say that the Fallen don't need a *reason* to steal and destroy."

By the time he'd seen to the last of the wounded, Prissie's emotions were in a weary tangle. The senselessness of the enemy's attacks angered her, the pain of the wounded defenders sickened her, and the threat of further violence frightened her.

Gently extracting the last roll of bandages from her hands, Padgett said, "Do not dwell on fear."

She looked up at him, and her lip trembled. "There's so much more than I knew about."

"And there is far more than this," he rejoined. "May that knowledge stir your heart to greater faith."

"But ... if I forget?"

"Then the memories will be stored up for you like treasures in heaven," he replied.

"R-really?" she mumbled, surprised when relief brought tears to her eyes.

Padgett held her gaze and gravely declared, "Nothing is lost for those who are found."

"Are you sure?" she asked with a sniffle.

"Quite sure," he promised. "You do not hope in vain. When the time for partings has ended, your joy will be full."

"I guess that's okay, then."

Padgett gently pulled her into an embrace. "Close your eyes." Her lashes fluttered shut, and the last thing she remembered was his voice speaking a simple benediction in her ear. "Sleep in peace, Prissie."

"You okay, Prissie?" whispered April. "You seem really out of it today."

She snapped to attention. "I'm fine, thanks."

April Mayfair peered steadily at her through the lenses of her rectangular-framed glasses, then shrugged. "If you say so."

Turning her attention back to the front, Prissie was relieved to see that Miss Knowles hadn't noticed her inattention. She wasn't usually the type to zone out in class, but she couldn't seem to corral her thoughts today. Her concentration was shot, so even though it was irresponsible, she gave up, promising herself to ask Koji about the lecture later on.

He was as meticulous a note-taker as she normally was, living up to his angelic order as a future archivist of heaven. His notes were a faithful record of their class periods, even if he did tend to stray off topic. Mixed in with the facts, figures, and formulas were snatches of praise, often in a language she couldn't read. Prissie thought this alone might have given away his true nature, but Koji didn't stop there. Unlike other kids their age, he didn't doodle in the margins; he *illuminated* them. All along one side of his notes, he added intricate illustrations that he later showed to Shimron, his mentor.

Prissie snuck a quick peek in April's direction, wondering if she'd noticed Koji's latest pen-and-ink masterpiece. Normally, her nose-for-news friend was quick to pick up on unusual things and even quicker to follow up on her hunches. If anyone was going to figure out the truth about Koji's heavenly citizenship, it would be April. But so far, she hadn't shown any signs of suspicion. Either April had written off his strange quirks as cultural differences, or she was providentially oblivious to the boy's inability to completely fit in with the rest of the class.

Koji sat at the desk in front of Prissie's, head bent as he worked. His black hair was gathered in a neat ponytail at the nape of his neck, and his slim shoulders were hunched over his notebook in a way that made her suspect he was drawing. She hoped he would show her after class. He usually did.

It was just a little embarrassing to think that her best friend at school was a boy. For weeks she'd worried that people would get the wrong idea about her and Koji; after all, they'd been quick to assume the worst about her and Marcus. But no one seemed to think that she and the young angel were an item, and Prissie was grateful. Those kinds of rumors would have spoiled something she never wanted to give up.

The very next day, Beau caught her attention in the hallway at lunchtime and pulled her aside. "Say, Prissie ... have you been hearing stuff?" he asked pensively.

"What do you mean?" she asked, her gaze following Koji, who continued into the cafeteria without her.

"People are saying stuff again."

"More gossip?" Prissie felt her stomach drop. "Is it about me and Koji?"

"No. It's about you and Margery."

She hadn't expected that. Shaking her head in confusion,

she asked, "What possible rumor would there be about us? Everyone knows we've been friends forever."

"Not lately," Beau pointed out.

"Obviously, but that's hardly my fault," she retorted in exasperation.

"I know," her brother replied, rubbing the back of his neck. "But some people are saying that you've been spreading rumors about her."

"What are these so-called rumors I'm spreading?"

"Dunno, Sis."

Prissie shook her head. "Who would believe something that vague?"

"I just thought you should be prepared. I didn't want you to find out in a way that puts you on the spot."

"Well, thanks."

Beau shrugged and slouched into the cafeteria, aiming for the table where he and his friends always sat. No new gossip had reached her yet, but she spent almost all of her time with Koji, so why would it? Mystified, Prissie lifted her chin and whisked inside, finding a patient Koji waiting for her just beyond the doors. Now that she was aware that there might be a problem, she noticed a few looks in their direction, although that could have been coincidental. Taking a deep breath, she led the way to their usual table.

Conversation screeched to a halt as soon as they walked up. Red flags waved furiously. Elise and Jennifer were all smiles, but Margery and April were avoiding eye contact. It was *definitely* a bad sign. Prissie and Koji sat down anyway and ate in awkward silence.

Later, Prissie caught up to April between classes. "Is there something going on that I should know about?"

April smoothed her hand over her sleek bob. "It might be better if you didn't," she said bluntly. "It's just talk."

"What kind of talk?"

April sighed. "It doesn't matter, Prissie. Leave it alone, and it'll blow over, just like the Marcus thing."

"I thought we were friends," Prissie said quietly.

"Yes, but I'm friends with Margery, Jennifer, and Elise too. I don't want to choose sides."

The bell rang, and April bolted, leaving Prissie in the lurch. One of the main reasons the rumors about her and Marcus had blown over was because both of them had been quick to set everyone straight. How could she defend herself if her friends didn't back her up? April *knew* the truth, but she wasn't willing to take a stand. By remaining neutral, she was letting the injustice continue. Deep down, Prissie felt that by doing nothing, April had actually condemned her.

4

THE ADVENT SERVICE

"What is their goal?" asked Jedrick in rising frustration. He paced the floor of the circular room where he often sought counsel.

"Do they need one?" Shimron challenged. "The Tower is here; that alone provokes them. The Fallen would make rubble of anything God has established."

The Protector shook his head. "What God has established, none can break!"

"Amen and amen."

With a frown, Jedrick pointed out, "The Deep is *not* impenetrable."

"And the Gate?" asked the old Observer.

Jedrick sighed. "Many have sought it; few could find it."

"Few?" Shimron echoed, then a thoughtful expression

crossed his face. "Ah, I see what you mean. There *are* those who can enter secret places, who open a way even when there is no door."

"A Caretaker," his captain confirmed. "Padgett has been targeted, but the enemy's snares are useless. Against one of his order, they are thoroughly outmatched."

The ancient archivist slowly laid aside his pen, his expression grave. Turning from his worktable, he crossed to one of the many bookshelves that lined the room and selected a gray volume with a spine decorated with the links of a chain.

Jedrick watched him with curiosity and concern. "What is it, Shimron?"

"There *is* one way," the old Observer said, his tone heavy with warning. Fixing his faded blue eyes on Jedrick, he asked, "How many Caretakers Fell?"

"I do not know," the Protector confessed. "It was before my beginning."

With a small sigh, Shimron spread wide the pages of his record and gently turned the pages. "Four Fell, and those four were scattered to the four corners of the earth, confined to the deep places until the last days." Arriving at the section he was seeking, the old Observer murmured, "I thought so."

The Protector's shoulders squared, as if braced for a blow. "Tell me."

Tapping the record, Shimron announced, "We stand upon one of those four corners."

Prissie *should* have been focusing on her homework, especially since assignments had piled up during her absence, and midterms were right around the corner. Instead, a dozen other little worries were using up her attention. Rumors—or rumors of rumors, actually—were circling, and she couldn't imagine what had set them off, let alone what was being said.

She and Koji sat at the kitchen table, and Prissie could tell by the rhythmic scratch of his pencil that he was drawing. Jude had lent Koji a box of crayons, and she'd offered up a jar of colored pencils. Surrounded by the tools of his trade, the young Observer actually reminded her a little of his mentor.

The absolute concentration on Koji's face lifted with a blink, and he met her gaze. Smiling softly, he announced, "The mail is here."

It took a few minutes before the muffled shouts of her younger brothers heralded Milo's arrival. He left his boots by the door and padded through to the kitchen in stocking feet. Draping his jacket over the back of a chair, he slid into it with a contented sigh. Miraculously, none of the other Pomeroys joined them. Or perhaps it was *providentially.* Prissie had noticed that happened fairly regularly where angels were concerned. "Hello," she greeted shyly.

Milo slid a box across the table. "This one's got your name on it, Miss Priscilla."

Her eyes widened. "Is it something important?"

He chuckled. "I'm sure it *is*, but it's not a message from on high. To be honest, I'm here because someone *else* was eager to see you."

"Who?" she asked, mystified. Before he could answer, little Omri burst into view and whizzed around her head in a dizzying display. She gasped in delight and spread her hands wide, offering them as a landing pad for the yahavim. With a flutter of translucent wings and a flick of his long, yellow ponytail, he alighted on her palm. Prissie's hands curved protectively around him as he took a seat and blinked at her with faceted eyes. "Hello, Omri," she crooned. She had to squint to see his smiling face, so great was his happiness.

"He was *very* insistent," Milo remarked.

"He can't talk," she countered. "How could he *insist*?"

"Even without words, Omri is clever enough to make himself understood," Milo said.

"I'm sure you are," she whispered. Prissie dragged her eyes from her cute little visitor to smile at the mailman, only to discover that another place at the table had been filled. "Hello, Taweel."

The big Guardian grunted a quiet greeting. For a moment, his smoky purple eyes met hers, but the fierce warrior bashfully looked away.

Almost immediately, Prissie noticed the bandages encasing his wrist. "Oh, no! You're hurt?" she exclaimed.

Meeting her gaze more squarely this time, he gruffly said, "Do not fear. It is mending well."

"But how did it happen?" she persisted, staring fixedly at oddly familiar gauzy material that looked as if it'd been woven from threads of light.

The Messenger and Guardian exchanged a glance, and Milo rubbed a hand over the top of his head. "I suppose you could say things have been busy around here lately."

Tapping the kitchen table with her finger, Prissie asked, "*Here*, here? Or just sort of ... around here?"

Koji interjected, "Do you remember where Padgett turned us aside when April was visiting?"

Prissie nodded slowly. "Sure, out in the back forty."

"That is close to ..." He trailed off, glancing uncertainly at his teammates.

"Close to an area that's become a battlefield," Milo smoothly supplied.

"Were you trying to get to Ephron?"

Taweel answered, "No. My place is here, with the rest of the Hedge."

"Unless you're Sent?" she pressed.

"Yes."

"But you *haven't* been."

The Guardian shook his head, then clarified, "At Jedrick's request, I regularly accompany Milo."

Prissie pursed her lips, then sighed gustily. "I wish everyone was safe."

Again, glances were exchanged, but before another word was spoken, Mr. Pomeroy wandered out of the small niche off the kitchen where he did his bookkeeping. He only worked half days on Wednesdays, so he'd been puttering around the house. "Afternoon, Milo," he greeted. "Can I offer you some refreshment? I have a cake cooling, though I should warn you of the risks. A new recipe and pint-sized *sous* chefs were involved!"

"Thanks, sir. I'd be happy to serve as guinea pig!"

Prissie's father reached for an apron, then cocked a brow at his daughter. "Why don't you pour our good friend a glass of milk while I serve?"

From his tone, Prissie knew she was being scolded for not offering anything sooner, and with a self-conscious glance at her visible and invisible guests, she hastily excused herself from the table. Omri tagged along to the refrigerator. He stood on her shoulder, hanging onto her ear, much as he did with Taweel. It was impossible not to smile with such a bright little companion.

"So who's the package for?" inquired Mr. Pomeroy as he cut into a cake that smelled of spice and oranges.

Prissie carefully placed a glass of milk in front of Milo, and he gave her a wink before answering, "This one's Miss Priscilla's."

"From Ida?" her father asked as he ambled over.

"Obviously," Prissie replied, going to the kitchen drawer for a pair of scissors.

Jayce peered at the postmark. "Kenya this time. Sis sure gets around!"

After marrying, Uncle Loren had whisked Prissie's precious aunt away, but Ida did her best to stay close by mailing postcards and packages from their various ports of call. Sometimes the boxes were for Grandpa Pete and Grandma Nell, and sometimes there were shipments for all the Pomeroys. But every so often Prissie was singled out. She and Aunt Ida had been close, "bestest" friends since they were the only girls in the family.

Snagging a slice of cake for himself, Mr. Pomeroy joined the rest at the table and nodded toward the box. "Go on, Princess. Let's see what she's been up to."

Ida always sent interesting things, and Prissie's mind skipped through possibilities while she cut through the paper and tape. Inside, she found a letter in her aunt's distinctive, loopy penmanship. Although she was enormously curious about the multicolored cloth under the folded sheet of paper, she took the time to read it first. "Oh," she murmured, glancing at her dad. "Auntie says she can't make it for my birthday, either. It'll probably be spring before they're back."

He nodded. "They don't always have much control over their schedule."

"I know." She skimmed the rest of the letter. "Maybe in time for apple blossoms, she says."

"Pretty colors," Koji remarked, his eyes fixed on the fabric peeping out of the box.

Turning her attention back to the package's contents, she carefully lifted out the cloth bundle. It was loosely knotted, so she undid the ties and gently folded back a corner. "Wood," she murmured, pulling out a carving, then passing it along for Koji to see. The first was a donkey, the next a sheep, and then an ox. By the time a shepherd and wise man joined the growing throng, her dad piped up, "It's a nativity set!"

Milo smiled faintly as he inspected the little wooden Gabriel. "These are handmade."

"By local artisans," Koji read from the small printed card that was with the figures.

Prissie arranged the figures on the table, smothering a giggle as Omri tilted his head and reached out to pat a wooden camel on its nose. Taweel's countenance was gentled by fondness as he beckoned to the tiny angel, who seemed bent on getting into mischief.

Catching his daughter's expression, Jayce commented, "Ida's always been good at this sort of thing."

"Finding unique gifts?" Milo hazarded.

With a grin, Prissie's father replied, "Making my girl smile."

That evening the Pomeroys piled into the van for the half-hour drive down into Harper. Deo Volente, which was mostly known as the DeeVee, was holding special midweek services for Advent, and Jayce and Naomi had decided to take the whole family.

Tonight was the second in a series of four, and Prissie was pretty excited. She'd stayed home last week because she had been sick, and since she'd missed the last *Messiah* rehearsal too, it felt like *forever* since she'd seen Baird and Kester, two more angels from Jedrick's Flight. Baird led worship at the popular church that met in Harper's elementary school gymnasium, and his apprentice Kester Peverell was a member of his band.

When the Pomeroys trooped through the doors of the school building, they were quickly overtaken by a throng of people with rosy noses and high spirits. Baird was in the thick of things and hard to miss with his red hair, candy-cane striped scarf, and bright green earmuffs. Spotting them, he waved furiously and waded over. "Oh, wow! You guys should have been here an hour ago! You coulda come with us!" he greeted.

Prissie was totally confused, but Tad asked, "For the caroling?"

"That's right!" Baird exclaimed. "'Tis the season to tromp through the neighborhoods around here. It's our weekly pre-advent service caroling extravaganza!"

"Might be fun," Neil remarked, glancing curiously at their parents.

"You better believe it's fun!" With a coaxing air, the redhead added, "We're going again next week."

Mr. Pomeroy traded a look with his wife, then nodded. "You lot could use the second car and get a head start on the rest of us," he offered.

"Weather permitting," their mother cautioned.

"Man, that'd be amazing!" Baird said, sidling over to Prissie. Even in his bizarre, furry boots, he wasn't any taller than her, so he was able to look her in the eye. "You should come," he said in a low voice. Giving her hand a quick squeeze before releasing it, the enthusiastic redhead broadly announced, "I need to finish warming up so I can warm up! I'll see you inside!"

As he pushed back into the crowd, spreading cheer with every exclamation, Prissie shook her head, still trying to fit the Worshiper's vibrant personality into her idea of what heaven might be like. He kept mixing her up by messing with her ideals, but she couldn't quite hold it against him. Baird was just … Baird.

When service time rolled around, the overhead lights in the gym were doused so thousands of tiny white lights could twinkle from the groups of artificial trees set up on either side of the stage. Prissie sat up a little straighter as the band members filed into their usual places. Baird himself stepped to center stage and stood quietly, his hands folded prayerfully over his blue guitar. Talking dropped to whispers, then ebbed to a soft rustle of movement. Once the room held nothing but an expectant hush, he closed his eyes and opened his mouth.

"Of the Father's love begotten, e'er the worlds began to be …" he began, his clear tenor filling the gymnasium.

Prissie didn't recognize the song, but her mother's soft sigh suggested that it was familiar to some.

"He is Alpha and Omega. He the Source, the Ending He … " Baird sang, continuing an especially lovely description of Jesus.

As the second stanza began, the low thrum of Kester's cello joined the song, sending a shiver through Prissie. Now

Baird seemed to be singing a duet with the stringed instrument's long, mellow notes. "O, ye heights of heaven adore Him; angel hosts, His praises sing ..."

Having a song that talked about angels being sung by an actual angel made Prissie's heart do flip-flops. It was perfect, and she found herself blinking back tears.

"Let no tongue on earth be silent, every voice in concert sing, evermore and evermore!" Making the lines an invitation, Baird raised his hands as the words to the next verse appeared on the overhead screen.

Prissie was delighted to learn such a beautiful song, and she was even gladder when Baird ushered them right back to the beginning so everyone could sing through the whole thing again. As the last *evermore and evermore* faded, he struck a chord on his guitar, and the drums began to thump in time to the beating of her heart. Kester moved over to the keyboard, and the rest of the band joined in, leading the congregation into another song of praise.

When the final chorus drew to an end, the DeeVee's pastor jogged lightly up the steps onto the stage, Bible in hand. Dennis Kern was a compact, charismatic man in his early thirties with dark hair and wire-rimmed glasses. He shook Baird's hand in passing, then turned to the audience. "Amen?" he asked. Dozens of answering *amen*s rang out, something that never would have happened in Prissie's home church. Wanting to support her friends, she did offer a firm nod.

Another thing that wouldn't have happened at First Baptist Church was Pastor Kern's sweater. Prissie hardly knew what to make of it. Over the last few months, they'd attended evening services at the DeeVee often enough for her to get used to a much more casual dress code. However,

Pastor Bert's wife Laura *never* would have let her husband into the pulpit in a bright red sweater with a big, waving snowman on it. It was outrageously festive, and it didn't take long to realize that his microphone really was picking up a soft tinkling noise. "Are those jingle bells?" she whispered to Koji.

The young Observer nodded solemnly. "There are six. They seem to represent the snowman's buttons, although I do not understand their function, since the snowman has no raiment whatsoever."

"That's hardly the point!" she muttered in scandalized tones.

Meanwhile, the pastor was casually running through some introductory remarks. "As many of you already know, we're in the midst of a Christmas sermon series called 'Naughty or Nice.' A lot of people, whether they mean to or not, think of God pretty much the same way they think of Santa Claus. If we're good boys and girls, we get the blessings we deserve, but if life's lumpier than a sock full of coal, it must mean we're in the wrong column on the Big Guy's list."

Prissie frowned over the man's casual approach to Bible teaching, but she had to admit he was easy to follow.

"Last week, we chatted about the stuff that lands us in trouble, the *thou shalts* and the *thou shalt nots.* But this week, I'm going to address something that's trickier to pin down. Instead of *dos* and *don'ts,* we're going to look at *didn't dos.* If we want to get fancy about it, we're moving from sins of commission to sins of omission." With a wry smile, he asked, "Have I lost you yet?"

It was going a little over Prissie's head, and she jiggled her foot impatiently. But Koji's fingers gently touched her hand.

Leaning nearer, he softly urged, "Do not just hear his words. Listen."

She gave her "conscience" an injured look. But when she tried to pull away, the young angel gave her hand a friendly squeeze. Turning her eyes to the front, Prissie tried harder to understand what the pastor was saying.

Dennis Kern was asking, "Have you ever forgotten something?"

Prissie sat up a little straighter.

"Not on purpose, of course," the pastor assured. "In fact, it was probably something small—a phone call you meant to make, an offer to pray for someone that never quite happened, a casual promise that's suddenly inconvenient to keep." He waved his hand. "Small things. Inconsequential. I can hear you now, saying 'It's no big deal, Denny. Don't sweat the small stuff!' But before you shrug off the things we let slide, let me ask you this: how do you *know* they weren't important?"

Prissie tried not to fidget, but it wasn't easy. She *already* knew that little things could be positively providential. God used them all the time around her angelic friends. What's more, she *didn't* need to be told she was forgetting something. She'd *admitted* that! Still, she was willing to keep listening if it would clear up the divine message she'd received.

The pastor went on. "Have you ever bitten your tongue when you knew you should have spoken up? Have you ever slouched a little lower in your seat when you should have taken a stand? I know I have, and afterward, I was plagued by a whole mess of coulda-shoulda-wouldas! Now, I'm not saying that as Christians we need to be ever-ready do-gooders. But I am saying that we can't hope to please God if we're a bunch of do-nothings!"

While he waited for that to sink it, Pastor Kern flipped open his Bible, casually glanced at a passage, then continued. "The Bible urges us to turn the other cheek, not to turn a blind eye. We may all agree that turning our back on someone in need is naughty, but is it easy to turn aside from our own plans in order to do the nice thing?" Scanning the audience with a small grin, he added, "And while I'm trying to turn another phrase, you may as well turn with me to...."

A ripple of amusement filtered through the gymnasium, and the lights came up so people could see their Bibles. Prissie followed along and heard him out, but by the time Pastor Kern was winding up, she wasn't any clearer on what Milo's message meant for her. Glancing guiltily at Koji, she wondered if her friend would be disappointed in her.

When she tuned back in, Pastor Kern was saying, "Put simply, there's the naughtiness of doing wrong, and there's an equally naughty sin of neglect, of not doing what's right. Nobody wants to be caught red-handed, but in the eyes of the Lord, it can be just as bad to be caught empty-handed."

Prissie knew she wasn't getting something, and she knew it was important. However, she was glad that one way or another, God had made sure her hand wasn't empty. Giving Koji's hand a squeeze, she felt a little better when he squeezed back.

5

THE PROTECTOR'S LESSON

That Hedge needs clipping," grumbled the lumpish figure lurking behind a dumpster.

"Be my guest, Murque," his companion replied smoothly.

Drawing his wicked blade, the demon growled, "Say the word, my lord."

"Not just yet," Adin murmured. "We'll give them time to grow lax. Let them believe they have thwarted us."

"Believing in lies, that's what." Murque's beady eyes squinted at the rooftop of the bakery. "Too bad you didn't snatch her at Halloween."

"Yes," Adin replied darkly. "Next time."

With a malicious smirk, the demon pushed his luck. "Bet you didn't expect to find a First One haunting the alley that night."

Adin frowned. "That meddler is cleverer than he seems."

"Seems a fool to me," countered Murque. "Strolling into danger without so much as a dagger."

"And *yet*, you fled," his lord mocked.

"So bright!" the cringing demon complained. "*Too* bright, and that *song*!"

Adin's expression hardened, and he whirled, stalking back the way they'd come. "Yes," he conceded in tones of disgust. "Driven before the light like the shadows we are."

After school on Friday, Prissie and Koji hightailed it from the bakery over to The Curiosity Shop for a visit. "Harken, can we talk?" she asked as soon as the pleasantries were out of the way.

"Of course, child. What's on your mind?"

She huffed in frustration. "I'm not sure!"

With a deep chuckle, Harken commented, "That's not as uncommon as you might think. Why don't you start talking? Perhaps, you'll work your way closer to the heart of your concerns."

"But where do I start?"

Flashing a broad smile, he suggested, "Let's start by going into the garden. Gardens are good places for beginnings."

"Yes, please!" Prissie replied, brightening considerably. She'd come to love the ornately carved blue door in the back room of Harken's store, for it led to a secret place that was bathed in heaven's own light. Turning the glowing door knob, she slipped right out of time and into a forest glade where it was always summer.

Following Koji's example, she took off her jacket and

boots, folding them neatly before laying them aside. It was exhilarating to be able to shed layers in the middle of winter, but she resisted the urge to flop in the grass like Koji did. It would have been undignified.

A sudden *crack* and *clang* sounded overhead, making Prissie jump. She quickly searched for the source of the sound. "It is easier to watch if you lie down," Koji said, beckoning for her to join him.

In the past, even when other angels were here, this place had been hushed and serene. Today was the first time that something else was going on. Sitting down and smoothing her skirt over her legs, Prissie asked, "Are they fighting?"

"Young Marcus often takes his lessons here," Harken explained.

Looking up into the seemingly endless swirl of light overhead, she watched in awe as two angels wheeled. Jedrick's wings flashed with emerald hues as he dipped and whirled with amazing agility. Marcus circled above him and dropped toward his sparring partner. Swords glinted, and another metallic crash rang out.

Prissie leaned back on her elbows, intrigued by the display. After a while, she noticed a pattern to the aerial dance, for the golden-winged angel seemed to be making mistakes. Then she realized that Jedrick was demonstrating, and Marcus was mimicking. This was a Protector's lesson on how to fight midair.

She was impressed in spite of herself. Marcus acted as if it was nothing to swoop and pivot high above the ground. Offhandedly wondering if she'd still be afraid of heights if she could fly, Prissie asked, "Do you ever wish you had wings?"

"No. I am content as I am," Koji replied.

"Lots of people wish they could fly like a bird," she remarked. "Or that they had super powers or magical abilities."

"I wish to please God," the young Observer answered seriously. "For that, I have only to do what I have been made to do. Besides, if I wanted to fly, I could simply ask Harken."

"I've been known to give rides to young friends," acknowledged the Messenger, who'd joined them on the grass.

"It must be nice in a way, not having any choice," Prissie mused aloud.

"In what sense?" inquired Harken.

"Well, Koji is an Observer, so as long as he's observing, he's doing what he should. You're a Messenger, so you deliver messages ... right?"

"Regularly," he agreed with a warm smile.

"It's different for me," she complained. "People are really relieved that Neil's figured out what he wants to be when he grows up. Since I'm next in line, they're starting to ask me if *I've* thought about the future."

"And you can't answer them?"

"No," she sighed, her eyes fixed on the sky. "I don't like to think about growing up and moving away. Everything will change."

"That's a ways off," the shopkeeper soothed.

"Tad, Neil, Ransom, April ... even Jude knows exactly what he wants to do when he grows up," she argued.

"Circumstances led to Neil's decision, and Jude's plans are natural enough," Harken said. "It may be that your circumstances will lead you toward the future God has in store."

"What kind of circumstances?" Prissie asked suspiciously.

"Usual ones. Unusual ones. Who can say?"

"We are circumstances," Koji declared.

Prissie's expression softened. "Unusual ones."

"The things you experience today help shape your understanding of tomorrow," Harken added.

"Head's up, kiddo!"

She glanced skyward only to duck with a squeak of alarm as Marcus zoomed in low over their heads. The young Protector's blade was sheathed, so it wasn't as if he was attacking, but Prissie still glared for all she was worth as he landed a short distance away. He tossed a casual wave their way, but a sharp call from overhead brought his attention back to his mentor. In a flash, he drew his sword and raised it to meet Jedrick's heavy blow.

"Footwork," the Flight captain chided.

With a short nod, Marcus dug in with his boots, and they returned to fighting, this time on the ground. The broad-shouldered Protector brought his blade to the ready and waved his apprentice forward, encouraging him to go on the offensive. With a surge of golden light, the younger angel charged. Prissie thought it strange to see a guy who'd just been slouching through the halls at school with a backpack hanging from one shoulder now lunging and slashing with a blade that looked sharp enough to do some serious damage.

Jedrick remained calm in the face of the attack. His muscular arms made the large sword with the blue gem in its pommel seem light, even though Prissie knew it had to be heavy. Marcus's sword was neither as long nor as broad, but it was a deadly enough weapon, reminding her once again that there were enemies outside of this place, dangers she could only imagine ... and didn't want to think about.

The memory of a starry sky filled with warriors flitted

across her mind's eye, but Harken chimed in then, inquiring, "So is that what you wanted to talk about today? The future?"

She slowly shook her head. "No, not really. It was something about Milo's message."

"Was my apprentice unclear?" the Messenger inquired lightly.

"I understood *him*," Prissie quickly assured. "It's the *message* I don't understand."

Harken gestured for her to continue. "What was the message?"

"Trust, listen, and remember," she listed.

The old man tapped his chin. "Listening may be the most difficult of the three."

"I'd think it was the easiest!"

"Yes, it *sounds* easy enough," Harken agreed. "It's like ... have you ever had trouble paying attention in class? Your mind strays, but the teacher hasn't stopped talking. Their words flow right past, but in your distraction, you're tuning them out."

With a faint blush, she replied, "I guess."

"That's the difference between *hearing* and *listening*," he explained.

Koji interjected, "Shimron says it is as important to listen wisely as it is to listen well."

Prissie's brow furrowed, but Harken nodded. "It can be difficult to sift the truth from lies." With a searching look, he restated, "You're unsure what you should be listening for ... and what you've forgotten ... but do you know whom you can trust, Prissie?"

Shrugging a little, she mumbled, "I trusted Adin."

"May I ask about him?" Harken inquired.

"I guess."

"What kinds of things did Adin say to you?"

She needed to think that over. It wasn't so much that she didn't remember what the fallen angel had told her; it was embarrassing to admit that she'd believed him. Adin had seemed so perfect. Very reluctantly, she confessed, "He said I was special, chosen by God."

"Arguably true." Harken nodded encouragingly. "What else?"

Prissie fiddled with her skirt, pleating the fabric between her fingers. "He talked about Ephron ... and Ransom ... and he asked questions I couldn't answer."

"Like?"

"Like ... why doesn't God hurry up and tell you where Ephron is? And why am I letting Ransom take my place next to Dad? And he asked me which of my brothers is my favorite."

Harken's expression grew solemn. "Did he, now?"

To Prissie's surprise, Koji grabbed her hand, pulling it into both of his own. "Adin stirred doubts, planted seeds of contention, and sought to divide Prissie from those who love her. I am grateful to God that we are Sent to her defense."

She didn't miss the subtle emphasis. "Who's been Sent? You two?"

"The whole Flight," Harken replied. "We're supporting Tamaes, which means looking out for you. Now! If you'll excuse me, I have a store to mind."

"Oh! Of course," she exclaimed, feeling bad for taking up his time. Prissie could see why her father had confided in Harken when he was her age. "Thank you for listening."

"Any time," he replied, making his reply a promise. "And stay as long as you like."

Since she wasn't in a hurry to go back out into the cold, Prissie basked in the warm light filling the forest clearing. As she'd once guessed, watching angels spar was much more interesting than football, but this wasn't just for sport. These two were cherubim, whose job it was to keep the Fallen at bay. Marcus was obviously young, but he was learning what he needed from his mentor. He was growing stronger through practice so that he could protect people like her.

A quick glance confirmed that Koji was avidly following every move, so she asked, "Do you understand what's going on?"

"Indeed."

"Could you use a sword, then?" she asked curiously.

"I have neither the strength nor the skill," he replied seriously. "And I am ill-equipped to defend myself." Marcus was blocking Jedrick's blows with his sword, and as she had noted once before, neither of them used any kind of shield. Just then, something happened that made Prissie lean forward. "What *was* that?" she whispered.

"Watch closely. They are sure to demonstrate again."

Sure enough, after a short interval, Marcus went on the offensive, swiftly launching himself at his mentor with sword upraised. Instead of bringing up his weapon, Jedrick's wings flashed forward, and to her amazement, they deflected the blow. "His wings!" she exclaimed. "He used his wings!"

"An angel's wings are a strong defense, shielding from blows of friend or foe," Koji recited. "They can also become a shelter from wind and weather, or a quiet place for healing and rest."

As she watched, the tables turned, and this time, Marcus's wings came around, the edges blending together in a seamless arc of light. "I never would have guessed," she murmured.

The Protector's lesson had already ranged from midair to a ground battle. Without warning, it changed again, and both angels were on the move. Prissie's jaw dropped as she twisted to follow the action. "What in the world … !" she exclaimed. Jedrick and Marcus still crossed blades, but in a crazy rush as they wove in and out between trees. Their heavy boots thudded over the grass, and they added tight wingbeats for bursts of speed. All the commotion shook leaves loose from the trees, and Marcus caused the slender trunk of a young sapling to bow by using it to change directions without slacking his pace. "Is this really training, or are they just showing off?"

Koji's gaze was solemn. "The enemy does not fight in an orderly manner. They ambush the unwary, give chase over great distances, and use any means possible to inflict pain upon their prey. Improvisation is often required to avoid grievous injury or capture."

To her, it looked like a playful game of chase, and she enjoyed watching in spite of the underlying purpose of their pell-mell blitz through the forest. Jedrick's attacks grew more ingenious, but Marcus seemed good at evasion, and before she knew it, Prissie was rooting for her classmate. "He's doing well, isn't he?"

"He is doing all he can," Koji agreed.

Finally, Jedrick called an end to the lesson and strolled over to where Prissie and Koji sat. After a moment's consideration, he chose a seat on the grass in front of the two, placing his sword within easy reach behind his back. Koji quickly crawled over to sit at the big warrior's side and was greeted by a gentle inquiry. "How have you been faring, my young Graft?"

Marcus also laid aside his weapon and dropped unceremoniously onto the grass. His wings were already hidden away, but when Prissie stole a glance in his direction, his eyes were still a vibrant shade of gold. He smirked in a friendly sort of way, but his attention went right back to Jedrick, who was asking Koji about recent additions to his responsibilities. The more they talked, the more Prissie realized that the big Protector genuinely cared about her friend. If this was Koji's family, then as captain, Jedrick was sort of like a father, making Marcus an older brother. It made sense to her, like how Jedrick teased Baird, and the way everyone in the Flight came together to support Tamaes.

"Prissie Pomeroy," the big Protector said slowly.

With a start, she wondered if he'd said her name more than once, for his eyes held a spark of amusement. Feeling foolish, she mumbled, "Pardon?"

"You are welcome to join us," Jedrick invited.

At first, Prissie wasn't sure what he was talking about, but she should have known. Somehow with angels, everything always ended up in song. She thanked him awkwardly. "You go on without me. I like to listen."

With a nod, Jedrick began to hum, and his two young teammates tuned their voices to his. The melody was simple, and the harmony was sublime. Marcus threw back his head and sang with unabashed enthusiasm, adolescence adding huskiness to his tones. Koji's voice was as clear and sweet as ever, and Prissie's heart swelled with an odd mix of pride and joy.

Now that the battle had ended, the yahavim flitted out from hiding. Prissie played with the little manna-makers while the trio of angels offered thanks and praise, and she was thrilled when the tiny angels added a melodious thrum to the chorus. Prissie found herself humming a few snatches every now and then, even though she didn't know the melody. She wasn't as talented as her companions, but she was glad. And the gladness just sort of spilled over. No one seemed to mind.

6

THE GIVING SEASON

Milo stretched his long legs and took in the view from atop the Pomeroys' barn while he waited for his teammate to rouse. The sun was just beginning to lighten the eastern horizon, but his shift at the post office didn't start for another hour or so. There was time enough for patience. Finally, Tamaes stirred, and the Messenger greeted him. "Good morning, sleepyhead. Pleasant dreams?"

The Guardian rolled to a sitting position and accepted the box of manna Milo proffered. "Ephron is the one who waits to be found, but I am the one who feels lost."

"Couldn't find him?"

Tamaes shook his head and gazed toward the rising sun. "Perhaps today will be the day."

"Amen," Milo agreed.

The mall parking lot was packed since there were only sixteen shopping days left until Christmas. Grandma Nell circled the lots while Grammie Esme sat tall, eyes alert for any sign of an opening. The latter whooped in triumph when they found a spot, then peered over her glasses at the young Observer in the back seat. "This is your first Christmas in the States, isn't it, Koji?"

"Indeed."

"Then you're in for a treat," she promised. "This is sure to put you in the holiday spirit! Isn't that right, Prissie?"

"Yes," she cheerfully confirmed. Grammie Esme had begged for a girls' day out, and Prissie had leapt at the chance … and successfully pleaded for them to include Koji in the shopping adventure. "It's so much fun!"

They hurried to the big mall entrance, where the automatic doors opened with a *whoosh* of warm, peppermint-and-pine-scented air. Inside, they were met by the hubbub of voices, and a subdued jingle of seasonal music played somewhere overhead. Koji drifted to a stop, his eyes darting in every direction, for there was a lot to see. Grandma Nell checked her watch. "Do you want to meet up in the food court in a couple hours? You can show him around, and then we'll take a break to grab a bite."

Prissie glanced at her friend, but the young Observer was too busy studying an oversized set of silver bells to offer an opinion. "Two hours, food court," she briskly confirmed. As her grandmothers bustled in the direction of one of the large department stores, Koji wandered closer to the glass wall that rimmed the second level's walkway. She followed, but only partway. He might be willing to lean out over the edge to admire the view of the skylights up above, but she wasn't going anywhere near that dizzying drop to the lower level. "What do you think?" she asked, raising her voice to be heard over the din.

Dark eyes flashed her way. "It is interesting," he replied. "There is light and color and even music."

"All good things!" she exclaimed, smiling happily over the festive feel in the air.

As Koji rejoined her, his fingers touched the back of her hand. Eyes on the crowds, he quietly said, "I do not wish to become separated."

She glanced around, wondering if anyone would notice or even care, then sighed. Did it matter what any of these strangers thought? She didn't want to become separated any more than he did. "We'll hold hands when it's busy."

"Thank you, Prissie," he accepted, fitting his fingers between hers and holding on tight.

"Are you nervous?" she asked curiously.

He shook his head. "There is so much to see, I believe I will become distracted. However, I do not wish to behave irresponsibly. My place is with you."

She smiled at his earnest admission. "We can walk slowly. I like seeing the decorations too, so it's no problem."

"Thank you," he repeated.

They strolled along, looking in huge windows plastered with ads for holiday discounts and gift ideas, which got her thinking. How did one decide what to give an angel for Christmas? The list of people she wanted to do something special for had expanded considerably this year. "What do you think Harken might like for Christmas?" she quizzed.

Koji shook his head. "I cannot say because I do not know."

"What about Tamaes? Or Baird?"

"There is nothing we need that God does not provide."

Prissie stubbornly argued, "But it's Christmas!"

"On that day, as any other day, our desires are the same."

"But I want to be able to give you a present!" she pressed.

Dark eyes blinked. "Me?"

"Obviously!" she grumbled. "You and just about everyone else in your Flight!"

Koji only shook his head in amazement. "We expect nothing."

"That's fine," she said briskly, eyeing a display of baubles on one of the many kiosks they passed. "Sometimes the nicest presents come as a surprise. They need to be perfect, though."

"Why do you insist on giving us presents?" he inquired curiously.

"Because ... because the wise men brought presents to baby Jesus!" she replied with a triumphant smile. He couldn't possibly argue with that.

Tipping his head to one side, the young angel asked, "Will you commemorate all other aspects of the events surrounding the birth of the Son of God?"

"Like what?"

"There was song," he replied, a hopeful light sparkling in his eyes. "Much song."

"Were you there?"

"No, that was before I was formed. But Harken told me about it. He was there."

"He was?" Prissie asked in amazement.

"Yes. He has told about many of the things he saw and learned while he was an apprentice," Koji explained. "It is good practice for me. Many of the records I make for Shimron have been tales of Harken's telling. His stories are vivid."

"Is that so?" she mused, pausing to admire a display of brightly painted nutcrackers. "It's hard to picture Harken being our age, but I suppose he must have been."

"Indeed." Koji leaned down to peer at the scene of a tiny village inside a snow globe. "He loves parables so much because he heard them firsthand."

"He knew Jesus?"

"Every angel knows Him," Koji said. "But, yes. Harken's mentor was close to the Redeemer while He walked the earth."

"Was he his Guardian or something? No, wait," she interrupted herself. "His mentor would have to be a Messenger too."

"That is correct," the young angel replied. "Harken's mentor was Gabriel."

Prissie was stumped. Scarves, hats, and gloves were pointless for an angel who didn't feel the cold. Plus, there wasn't a store in the world that carried clothes big enough for giant warriors like Taweel and Jedrick. And it seemed silly to get Harken a book when he owned an entire store full of them. "I wonder if there's any instrument that Kester doesn't have?"

"I do not know. Should I ask?" Koji offered.

"No, that would spoil the surprise." She frowned thoughtfully, then sighed. "I don't know what to get *anyone*! Maybe I could just bake for them again? But ... that might not be special enough."

As she rambled, Koji listened with a thoughtful expression on his face, but he offered no solutions. Finally, she huffed and glanced at her watch. "I guess it'll have to wait.

Something will come to me. Let's go! We only have an hour left, and I want to start looking for my ornament."

Koji had followed her in and out of some of the smaller shops, never complaining like her brothers might have. He seemed just as interested in the items lining the shelves as he was in the people perusing them. As she steered him toward one of the big stores anchoring the end of the mall, he asked, "Ornament? Are you seeking some form of adornment?"

"I think the word you're looking for is *accessory*, but no," she replied. "I'm talking about tree ornaments."

"Your brothers have spoken extensively about your family's Christmas traditions," Koji noted, reaching for her hand as they joined the throng of shoppers entering the department store. "I am to be afforded a sock of my own."

"Stocking," she corrected. "And *of course* you'll be included. You'll be added to our gift exchange too!"

"Yes," he confirmed. "Your mother already invited me to participate. I am interested to see how the lots shall be cast."

With such a large family, the Pomeroys didn't even attempt to have everyone choose gifts for everyone else at Christmastime. Instead, the siblings enjoyed an annual game of Secret Santa. Prissie shook her head in amusement. "We pull names out of a hat."

"Why do you require an ornament?" Koji asked.

"It's a tradition," Prissie proudly replied. "Grandma Nell started it with Aunt Ida when she was a girl, and they included me when I came along. Every year, she buys us one special ornament. We'll choose one for Auntie too, even though her collection is in the attic right now."

"I see."

"This way," she said, pointing confidently at the small forest of artificial trees just ahead. "Sometimes, Auntie sends me ornaments too. She knows just the kind that I like best, so they're always really beautiful. Oooh, pretty!"

Prissie let go of Koji's hand as they reached the store's impressive display of seasonal ornaments. She drifted between trees of different heights, eagerly inspecting the offerings. He trailed after her, but soon became distracted by the incredible variety. She nearly ran into him when they both circled the same tree in opposite directions.

"There is much to see, but I do not understand the purpose of many of these adornments." Koji pointed uncertainly to a tree decorated entirely with birds. "I do not see how this connects with the Savior's birth. Is this a celebration of the fifth day of creation?"

She laughed softly. "It doesn't really have anything to do with *anything*," she explained. "Some people collect ornaments according to a theme."

"Like you?" he asked.

"Well, sort of," she conceded. "I've always chosen ornaments that I really liked, and they're all different shapes and sizes. But most of them are colored glass ... like this." Prissie pointed helpfully to a glass sphere with swirls of pink and gold covering its surface.

"Will you be searching for an ornament based on appearances again?"

She could tell there was a challenge lurking in his tone, and she impulsively took him up on it. "I think *this* year, I want an ornament that reminds me of *you*."

He blinked. "It is not the season of *my* birth."

Prissie gently touched a pink-frosted icicle before glancing his way. "Do you have a birthday?"

Koji hesitated. "I am not aware of the true date of my beginning, but I do know what day Abner chose for the papers I needed when becoming a Graft."

"What day?"

"The day I met you," he replied quietly.

Prissie's eyes widened. "Summer, then? It was the end of July."

"Indeed."

"I don't remember what the exact date was," she admitted.

"The twenty-fifth day of July," he supplied.

"I'll remember that!" she cheerfully promised.

"Why?"

She rolled her eyes. "Because we'll need to celebrate the day together ... *obviously*!"

Koji's expression softened. "That would bring me great joy."

Back in the food court with Prissie's grandmothers, she and Koji decided on pizza. They carried their tray of food back to the table where Grandma Nell and Grammie Esme were sitting with plates of Chinese takeout. As usual, the young Observer managed to fade into the background, letting the ladies visit while he contentedly chewed.

At first, the main topic of conversation was shoes. Grammie Esme wanted to buy Prissie a new pair to go with the Christmas dress that Grandma Nell had been working on since after Halloween. While her grandmothers debated the pros and cons of suede versus patent leather, Prissie glanced over to see if Koji was enjoying his food. As usual, he ate with concentration, and a smile snuck onto her face.

That's when Grammie chuckled. "Speaking of pairs ... you two are just so darn *cute* together! Aren't they adorable, Nell?"

"Are they?"

"Look at them!" Esme gushed.

Grandma Nell nodded but kept her tone even. "I can see them fine, beings as they're sitting right in front of us."

"Oh, you know what I mean!" scoffed the other woman, whose eyes were twinkling. "They look like they're *special* to one another!"

Prissie couldn't believe her own grandmother would do this to her. Then again, Grammie Esme did love to stir the pot. Still, the teasing made her uncomfortable. Grandma Nell never stood for nonsense, and to Prissie's relief, she came to her granddaughter's defense. "Is it so strange that these children have become friends? Honestly, Esme!"

"But she's at that age," Grammie countered, waggling her brows.

Prissie thought she might be on fire, her cheeks were burning so brightly.

"Excuse me," Koji spoke up, and all eyes swung his way. "Prissie *is* my friend, and I am pleased that you can tell so easily. That is as it should be."

Esme straightened her glasses. "You don't say?"

"I do say," the young angel calmly replied. "I will gladly confirm it, for it is the truth."

Grammie clapped her hands and laughed. "Well said! Doesn't he sound just like a prince, Nell? So chivalrous, coming to her defense like that!"

"He does have manners," Grandma Nell blandly agreed.

"Now about those shoes. Don't you think heels are too impractical this time of year? There's snow to contend with."

The conversation drifted back where it belonged, and Prissie breathed a sigh of relief. Koji reached for his drink, and she followed suit since her mouth felt too dry. Then he slid his foot over until it bumped hers. Her grandmothers were deeply entrenched once more, so they paid no mind when she sent Koji a cautious glance. With a small smile, he whispered, "Fear not."

Somehow, that was all Prissie needed to hear. She smiled back.

7
THE SKATING PARTY

An hour before dawn, Milo rapped lightly on the front door of a log cabin set back from one of the narrow roads that wound through Sunderland State Park's extensive grounds. Moments later, the door swung wide, allowing warmth and light to spill out onto the snowy steps. Abner peered sharply at the Messenger. "So it's you?"

"The lot has fallen to me," acknowledged his teammate.

Raising his voice, Abner called, "It's Milo!"

"I thought as much," Padgett replied mildly. "Only a Graft would enter through the front door."

Abner's eyes drifted out of focus, and he murmured, "A valid point ... or would you call that a keen observation? Hmm."

With gentle assertiveness, his apprentice invited, "Won't you come in?"

Once Milo was settled in a chair before the hearth, a veritable swarm of yahavim darting about his ears, Abner remarked, "Aril will be pleased to see you again. How long has it been?"

"Not since the beginning," the Messenger reminded.

The Caretaker straightened his glasses and demanded, "*Which* beginning? There have been many."

Milo chuckled. "You were newly arrived, and Jedrick was newly appointed."

Fluttering his fingers at the little manna-makers vying for his attention, Abner murmured, "Full circle? Perhaps, perhaps...."

Padgett cleared his throat and interjected, "Morning and evening for a fortnight. Find me whenever you're ready, and I'll open the way."

Milo nodded amiably. "I'll be looking forward to it."

Prissie fiddled with the tassels of her new scarf, trying to get them to lay right against her shoulder. The fussy accessory and its matching hat were early Christmas presents from Grammie Esme, who loved indulging her grandchildren. The set was more for looks than warmth, but Prissie adored the pearlescent sheen given off by their hundreds of tiny sequins. She'd dressed with care, but not for the boys from Zeke's Sunday school class who'd be arriving soon. Their teacher still had a way of making Prissie want to look her best, like a habit she couldn't quite break.

Giving her hair a fidgety pat, she sat with a flounce of heavy skirts on one of the makeshift benches beside their duck pond. Milo had approached the Pomeroys about bringing his third- and fourth-grade boys over on a Sunday afternoon for a rowdy sort of Christmas party. Dad had readily agreed, and Momma had offered to supply cookies and cocoa for everyone afterward.

The weather was perfect—overcast and not too cold, with the occasional drift of snowflakes in the air. Prissie took a deep breath and released it in a puff of warm mist. Today promised to be fun, and she could hardly wait for it all to begin.

Koji was reshoveling the path down from the barn while Neil gave the ice a final sweep. The hourglass-shaped pond with its red footbridge made a pretty setting for skating parties, not that they'd hosted one in quite some time. All of the older Pomeroys' friends had outgrown their skates and moved on to other things. Tad had long ago given up on skating, but Neil still liked it well enough. He skimmed around the edges of the pond with ease, gliding in a wide figure-eight as he inspected his handiwork.

Just then, Milo's voice hailed them from the gate up by the barn, and Prissie's stomach flip-flopped. No matter how many times she told herself that things were different, her heart insisted that the mailman was special. She cared about him in much the same way she cared about Koji. But these feelings were stronger, and it was hard to know what to do with them.

"Hey, Neil!" Milo called, strolling right to the edge of the ice. Prissie's brother zipped over and swooshed to a stop. A minute later, Neil was beaming under the mailman's compliments. Milo then ambled over and joined Prissie on the bench. "Hey, Miss Priscilla. I appreciate your willingness to lend a hand with the boys today."

"I don't mind helping," she replied, trying to hide her sudden bout of awkwardness.

He nodded and unslung the skates hanging from one shoulder by their laces, ready to trade his boots for blades. "I heard back from everyone, and it sounds like the whole class will be here."

"How many?"

"Eight, counting Zeke."

Relaxing some, Prissie remarked, "It's a small pond, but it's perfect for little kids. Zeke's really excited."

"Nearly as excited as Koji," Milo said with a chuckle. Nodding toward the ice, he inquired, "Have you already given it a go?"

"Nooo," she slowly admitted. "I was waiting."

"Take a turn with me?" he invited, standing and offering his hand like a gentleman.

A sudden sense of déjà vu swamped Prissie, for Adin had done the same thing when he'd tried to coax her out the back door of the bakery. He'd made her feel special, but news of his attention had been enough to make Tamaes shake and Koji beg her not to stray. If she'd taken the enemy's hand, something awful might have happened.

"No?" the Messenger asked, ready to withdraw his offer.

"Yes, please," she hastily agreed, allowing him to help her up. "You know, you're nothing like Adin."

His eyes widened for a moment, but then Milo smiled. "I'm glad to hear that, Miss Priscilla, but what brought him to mind?"

She hoped the cold was a good enough excuse for the color creeping into her cheeks. "He wanted me to take his hand."

"But you didn't," the mailman countered, tucking her arm through his and striking out across the pond.

"But ... I *wanted* to," she confessed quietly.

"Adin is especially dangerous because he's taken a personal interest in us," Milo replied seriously. He gave her mittened hand a pat. "It's astonishing that he got as close as he did, but don't be afraid. No matter what the future holds, we're with you."

They skated in silence for a few moments before Prissie said, "You're really good at this."

"Next best thing to flying," he replied with a wink.

"Oh! Is that why it comes so easily for you?" She was impressed with how confidently he skated, and it didn't take long for her to match his rhythm.

"No, I had to learn the hard way, just like anyone else. There's a rink down in Harper where Baird likes to take the youth, and I often join them." He guided her through a wide figure-eight before adding, "We'll need to help Koji along. I don't think he has any idea how difficult this is."

Prissie glanced at the benches where Neil was helping the young Observer lace into a pair of hand-me-down skates. While she watched, Koji stood and stepped cautiously out onto the ice, then sat down hard. With a giggle at his surprised expression, Prissie called, "Wait for me, Koji!" Milo released her so she could rush to her friend's side. "Are you okay?"

"I am unharmed," Koji assured. "However, I may require assistance."

Prissie offered her hands. "I'll help."

"Thank you," he replied earnestly, allowing her to haul him back to his feet. Immediately losing his balance, he windmilled his arms, then flung them around her waist. "This is much more difficult than it appears."

"It gets easier. You just need a little practice," she promised, bracing herself as Koji cautiously straightened. "Come on."

Prissie gripped his arms near his elbows, and he locked his fingers around her forearms, leaning forward as she skated backward, pulling him along. He wobbled badly, but his eyes sparkled with excitement. "You are skilled," he said breathlessly.

"Not really." She was pleased to have impressed him, but she hardly considered skating backward as skilled, especially since it was the extent of her abilities. Prissie actually thought *he* was the admirable one, for Koji threw himself into all these new experiences with wholehearted enthusiasm. He was an Observer, but watching wasn't enough for him; he treated these opportunities like precious things that shouldn't be wasted. "That's the way," she encouraged.

His brows drew together in concentration. "I do not know what to do."

"Just follow my lead."

"You are going backward, so I cannot emulate you."

"Oh ... good point," she conceded, then warned, "I'm going to let go for a second." With a quick swish and turn, Prissie came alongside her friend, linking arms as they made a clumsy circuit of one half of the pond. Koji's jaw had a determined set to it, and he was catching on, perhaps because he wasn't afraid to fall. "Some of the boys who are coming today will be just starting out too."

"Will you teach them as well?" he asked.

"That's one of the reasons Neil and I are here," she

explained. "Milo wants everyone to have fun, even the beginners."

Neil zipped by. He'd always loved going fast, so whenever he was on the pond, it became a speed-skating track. Prissie *tsk*-ed as Neil whipped past, bending low in order to clear the bridge and shooting through to the other side. "Hopefully, he and Zeke will be the only daredevils in the bunch. Otherwise, it's going to get a little crazy around here."

"Hey, Koji," greeted Milo as he meandered over in a series of graceful curlicues. "Have you found your feet?"

"Indeed, no," the Observer promptly replied. "I cannot do this on my own."

"Then it's a good thing that Miss Priscilla and I are here!" he exclaimed, slipping his arm through his teammate's. Quirking his brows at Prissie, he inquired, "Shall we give him a foretaste of ice skating glories?"

"Is that okay?" She gave Koji a worried look.

"Yes!" Koji begged. "Please?"

Milo exclaimed, "Ice skating is like flying with your feet on the ground!"

Again and again, they circled the near side of the pond with their student skater braced between them. Koji gradually lost his wobble, but he never progressed beyond a sort of shuffle. At the young Observer's urging, they picked up the pace, and on the count of three, ducked under the red footbridge.

They dug in to go faster, and Milo changed direction so often, their skating became a crazy dance. Koji tipped his face skyward and closed his eyes, clearly enjoying the feel of wind against his skin, and Prissie was almost positive that she could feel the brush of invisible wings as they wheeled and whirled across the ice.

Milo squeezed her shoulder to get her attention. "Let me try something?"

Nodding, she broke away from the two and skated to the edge where Neil watched with a half-smile on his face. "Grandpa's right," he said, jostling her with his elbow. "That kid knows how to enjoy life."

She nodded in agreement, watching curiously as Milo pocketed his gloves. Assured of a better grip, he and Koji grasped each other's wrists, and after a couple of quiet words, the Messenger began to spin. The whirl gained speed until Koji's feet lifted off the ground, with Milo anchoring him. Prissie chewed her lip worriedly, but everything seemed to be under control. In fact, the young Observer was so happy, he almost seemed to glow.

"Hoo boy," Neil said as he cast a quick look in the direction of the house. "If Zeke catches sight of that little move, Milo's gonna spend all afternoon spinning in circles."

Prissie was about to agree when an unexpected sound robbed her of words. From the midst of the whirlwind, a burble of excitement changed into rolling laughter. "Oooh," she breathed. Strange as it seemed, now that she thought about it, she'd never heard Koji laugh before.

Neil chuckled right along with him, but Prissie simply watched in amazement. She'd always loved Koji's rare smiles, and this was something she wanted to remember forever. Her own smile developed a wobble, for she sort of wished she'd been part of the reason her serious-natured friend couldn't contain his joy. Holding onto his and Milo's secret made her feel closer to them, but she longed for more. Mostly, she wanted to matter to them as much as they mattered to her.

Later that evening, Prissie and Koji sat on opposite sides of her bedroom working on homework. The door was propped open, but so far, her brothers hadn't made pests of themselves. Since it was chilly upstairs, she had an extra pair of socks on her feet and a blanket wrapped around her shoulders, but Koji barely noticed that the furnace didn't do a very good job of reaching Prissie's little sanctuary.

Closing her history book with a snap, she dropped it atop the pile of textbooks on the bed, and Koji glanced up. "Have you retained the records we were assigned?"

She tapped the eraser of her pencil against the notes she'd made. "Mostly. I'll review on the way to school tomorrow."

He nodded and went back to reading, even though he was several chapters ahead of the class in their textbook. Giving the end of her braid a little tug, she asked, "Did you have fun today?"

Koji looked up again, and this time, he let his book fall shut. "Indeed."

"I could tell. And I think Neil would have liked to try that spinning thing Milo did with you ... if it was physically possible."

"Milo is the fastest in our Flight, but he is not the strongest," Koji replied seriously. The young Observer's gaze took on a faraway quality before he blinked and focused on her again. "May I invite Tamaes to join us?"

Prissie looked pointedly toward the open door and lowered her voice. "We'll have to be careful what we say. My brothers sometimes snoop."

He nodded. "I will choose my words with care."

"Then yes, I'd like that." It felt like a long time since she'd last seen Tamaes, and the prospect was a nice one. "Is he close by?"

Koji simply pointed to the roof, and she stared up at the plain, white ceiling. "How does he get in?" she wondered. "He came through the bedroom door last time."

"At that time, Tamaes was already inside."

"So can he walk through walls or something?"

"No," Koji replied, frowning slightly. "He will enter through the way that has been prepared."

"There's no blue door in here," Prissie pointed out.

"The way between is given whenever we are Sent. I do not know how else to explain it."

"Maybe you should just show me."

"Tamaes will do so." His gaze swiveled upward.

A moment later, a circular patch on the ceiling rippled faintly, and with a sudden rush, a familiar figure dropped into the room. Tamaes landed in a crouch in the center of her braided rug and swiftly scanned every corner of the room before bashfully meeting her gaze. "Good evening, Prissie," he greeted in low tones.

"Hi," she returned in a soft voice, just in case anyone was in the hallway. "Is everything okay?"

The big warrior hesitated, then admitted, "That is a difficult question to answer. You are safe, and for that I am grateful."

"Tonight isn't a *quiet* night, is it?" she asked with a glance out the window.

"No," he replied solemnly. "However, there is no cause for you to fear."

Pulling her blanket more closely around her shoulders, Prissie said, "I'm glad you're here."

"I am never far," Tamaes pointed out.

Prissie understood that even though the battle was invisible, it was real and fierce, so she felt as though she was keeping her Guardian safe by keeping him close. She supposed that it was actually the other way around, but for the moment, it was reassuring to have Tamaes where she could see him. "Make yourself at home," she ventured.

"Thank you," he replied, undoing the clasp that held his sword in place between his shoulder blades. Without another word, he chose a seat on the floor below her window, stretching out his long legs and placing his sheathed weapon within easy reach.

She and Koji both turned slightly to include Tamaes, but there wasn't much else they could do with her whole family still up and about. In fact, Zeke chased Jude past the door, roaring like a mad beast while his little brother shrieked with laughter. Prissie frowned disapprovingly before whispering, "Do you want a book or something?"

"There is no need," Tamaes assured.

Staring in disbelief as her Guardian simply folded his hands in his lap and stared back, she quizzed, "Don't you get bored?"

This time, the big warrior seemed puzzled. But Koji leapt in to explain, "He cannot be bored if you are near."

"Me?"

"You are his occupation." Leaning closer, he gravely confided, "Abner calls you his *preoccupation*."

Tamaes made a small noise of protest. "I am a Guardian."

Prissie was amazed that both angels apparently thought this a satisfactory explanation. "But it'll be awkward if he just sits there staring at me," she argued. "He should do *something* other than twiddle his thumbs!"

The warrior glanced uncertainly between her and his thumbs. "What do you suggest?"

"Well ..." She cast about for a suitable response. "I doubt you can help us study."

"There *is* an assignment he can assist you with," Koji said.

She tapped the textbooks. "I'm pretty much done for tonight."

"Have you forgotten the reading Pastor Ruggles encouraged us to do on Sunday?"

Prissie blinked, thinking hard. "I guess so. What are you talking about?"

"In preparation for Christmas, he encouraged everyone to review those Scripture passages that foretold the coming of Messiah," Koji reminded. "Have you done so?"

"Nooo," she grudgingly admitted. "I figured it was optional."

The young Observer spread his hands wide. "And you now have the option to complete the assignment. Tamaes will speak the words."

Her Guardian inclined his head, indicating his willingness to go along with the plan.

"Well, I suppose that's fine. My Bible's right over there." A thought occurred to her, and she tentatively asked, "Can you read any language like Milo?"

"No, but there is no need. The words are here," Tamaes explained, placing his hand upon his chest.

"You know them by heart?"

"I do."

Prissie shook her head incredulously. "Are you trying to tell me that you have the whole Bible memorized?"

With a faint smile, Tamaes replied, "It is pleasant to dwell upon the words of God."

"Go on," Koji urged.

So the soft-spoken angel spoke at length, his voice filled with reverent authority as he recited entire passages from the psalms and the prophets. Prissie settled back against her pillows, somewhat awed, for the familiar words sounded different when spoken aloud and with such conviction.

If either angel thought it strange that all Prissie did was sit there, staring at Tamaes while slowly twiddling her thumbs, they did not mention it.

8

THE FINAL REHEARSAL

In a room where every wall and door was painted a different color, strands of rainbow-hued Christmas lights were tacked up along the ceiling. Baird sat cross-legged in the middle of a pile of beanbag chairs, humming as he moved his fingers across the frets of his blue guitar. He glanced up as the door opened, and Milo rapped on its frame. "You haven't eaten today," the Messenger scolded.

"No, I'm pretty sure I remember eating," the redhead countered.

"Sure about that?" his teammate inquired in teasing tones.

Baird eyed him suspiciously. "Did my apprentice send for you, by any chance?"

"He did!" Milo cheerfully confirmed. "According to Kester, all you've had today is a toaster pastry, a bag of potato chips, and a package of licorice. That's *not* exactly the food of angels."

"I'm a terrible cook?"

"Come aside and refresh yourself. You *need* to relax for a while." The mailman crouched before him and extended a small box. "Eat your manna, Baird."

With a short huff and a small grin, Baird accepted it, lifting the lid to reveal small wafers of condensed light. "Pull the shades for me?"

Milo was just lowering the last of them when the light in the room doubled, then trebled. Turning, he smiled at the sight his friend made. Kneeling in the center of the tiny apartment, Baird's outstretched wingtips just brushed the corners of the room, their glory outshining the festive twinkling of his holiday decorations. Hushed notes accompanied the rustle of stained-glass wings, and Milo's smile broadened as his eyes slipped shut. Heaven drew close when those born to worship gave thanks to God.

Prissie wondered if God would forgive her for hating Elise. Never in her life had she met someone so spiteful, and she heartily wished the girl would go back to wherever it was she came from. "What did I ever do to her?" Prissie begged miserably.

Koji handed her another tissue. "I am not aware of any offense."

"Did you hear what she said?"

"I did." He edged closer to her on the step. "She apologized immediately."

"She didn't mean it," Prissie said bitterly. "She *meant* to be mean."

During lunch, Elise had found so many ways to slight her,

subtly ridiculing everything from her bagged lunch to her unpierced ears. Prissie might have been able to brush it off if it hadn't been for her friends. None of them had come to her defense. No one had tried to change the subject. It was as if they agreed with Elise's cutting comments, and that knowledge was too much to bear. She'd excused herself politely enough and left the cafeteria with her head held high ... until she was in the clear. Then she fled, Koji close on her heels.

No one really used the stairwell where she was hiding, so she was a little surprised to hear a door open somewhere above them. For a moment, she held out a fleeting hope that April or even Margery had come to see if she was okay. But the voices that filled the echoing space were male, and she hid her face against her drawn-up knees. Hopefully, they would just ignore her.

The *galumph* of sneakers thudded closer, but when they reached the landing above her and Koji, they stalled. "Miss Priss?"

She groaned and covered her head with her hands. "Go away, Ransom."

Completely ignoring her words, he hurried down the last flight of steps. "Hey, Koji."

"Hello, Ransom ... Marcus."

Prissie's head came up, and she blinked in surprise at the Protector, who leaned against the wall with his hands in the pockets of his brown leather jacket. With an unhappy grunt, she went back to hiding a face that had to be red and puffy from crying. "Leave me alone," she ordered in a muffled voice.

Instead, Ransom crouched in front of her, a concerned expression on his face. "You feeling okay?"

"I'm fine."

He snorted. "Liar. What's going on?"

"Nothing," she stubbornly insisted.

"What's your verdict, Conscience?" Ransom inquired.

Koji pushed another tissue into Prissie's hand, giving it a covert pat. "Unkind words."

"Rumor mill still grinding?" he asked lightly. "I suppose this time it's tougher to shake the gossip since you can't exactly deny it."

Prissie peered warily at him. "What do you mean?"

Ransom made himself comfortable on the floor, sitting with legs crossed as he met her watery gaze. "Last time, they were saying stuff about you and Marcus, and none of it was true."

"Obviously," she muttered, casting a look at the angel with two-tone hair. Marcus was watching them closely, and for once, there was no smirking or sly remarks.

With a shrug, Ransom continued. "This time, it's not a flat-out lie."

"You know what they're saying?" she asked, dabbing self-consciously at her nose.

His brows shot up. "You don't?"

She slowly shook her head.

"Huh. Well, it's nothing weird or kinky or anything," Ransom explained. "It's actually kinda funny ... from my perspective."

Prissie glared for all she was worth, but that wasn't much right now. Her old nemesis was teasing her, but there wasn't a speck of meanness in his manner. She was in a position to tell the difference now. "Well?" she prompted sulkily.

With an ironic smile, Ransom revealed, "Elise has been making sly remarks about *people like you*."

A distant bell warned that lunch was over, and Prissie knew they'd need to make their way to their fourth-period classes soon. She didn't budge, though. It was confusing, being on the other side of the phrase she'd so recently flung at him. "Someone like me?" she whispered, shaking her head in confusion.

"Yep," he confirmed. "Basically, she's saying that you and your family are all religious fanatics."

Prissie stared at him blankly. "Wh-what?"

"You wouldn't believe some of the crazy stuff they're whispering about," said Ransom. "They're lumping you with every crackpot and charlatan in history, and if what they're saying is true, anyone would be a fool to consider becoming a Christian."

She couldn't believe it. Instead of telling an outright lie, Elise had simply twisted the truth into something ugly. How did you set people straight when their ideas were so skewed?

Ransom wasn't done. "So tell me, Miss Priss ... will you ditch the whole faith thing in order to fit in again?"

She gaped at him, stunned that he'd suggest such a thing. It wasn't even tempting. In fact, it was quite possibly the stupidest thing she'd ever heard. "Never," she gasped. Wrapping her arm tightly around Koji and cutting a sharp look at Marcus, she vehemently exclaimed, "Never, ever, *ever*!"

"Sure about that?" Ransom asked in teasing tones.

"Completely!" she retorted, her voice ringing.

Hauling himself to his feet, he nodded to himself. "Thought as much. You're your father's daughter after all. Good to know."

Ransom ambled toward the door, and Marcus pushed off the wall to follow. But first, he leaned down and gently flicked

Prissie's forehead. "Amen and amen, kiddo," he whispered before trooping after his friend.

After all the drama at school, Prissie was glad to immerse herself in something Christmassy. This was supposed to be the season of sugar plum fairies and gingerbread men, not gossip and persecution. "It's busy tonight," she whispered to Koji from their usual seat at the back of the balcony in the Presbyterian church. There were easily two hundred people in the pews below, for tonight was the final run-through of Handel's *Messiah* with the orchestra.

As the musicians warmed up their instruments, the choir practiced filing onto the stage, and the director explained to his soloists when to step forward and where to stand. Prissie spotted Kester in the strings section, drawing a bow across his cello and adding low, mellow notes to the rest of the tuning.

When the director stepped up to the podium, everyone gave him a round of applause, and then a hush fell as the first chords of the overture filled the sanctuary. Prissie squiggled down in her seat and closed her eyes, smiling softly. This had been a part of Christmas for as long as she could remember, and the strains were like the voice of a dear friend.

If she concentrated, she could pick out Harken in the bass section, and after the first several measures, Baird's electric guitar made itself heard. Koji sat straight and tall, his eyes taking in all that happened, but he wasn't ignoring her. As a shiver of excitement thrilled through her heart, his hand briefly touched hers. "I *love* this," she whispered.

"I understand why," he replied solemnly. "All have gathered to hear the Living Word proclaimed in song."

"They *are* all Bible verses, aren't they? I guess I knew that, but I think of them as songs."

"It is Milo's turn," Koji announced, nudging her with an elbow.

She quickly sat up and rested her arms on the back of the pew in front of them as the Messenger stepped into place and waited for his cue. "Comfort ye ... comfort ye My people...." His clear tenor rose confidently over his accompaniment, carrying all the way to the back.

"The song is perfect for Milo," whispered Prissie.

"It is indeed a Messenger's song."

Even with the changed pace of the classic, this solo remained a gentle ballad, and she loved hearing the good news proclaimed by one who lived to relay God's words to others. She doubted she would *ever* hear a more heartfelt performance.

"And cry unto her that her warfare, her warfare is accomplished," Milo sang.

A small part of Prissie's happiness dimmed, and she looked to Koji. "Will your war end?"

"It will."

"When?" she wondered.

"In the fullness of time," Koji replied as Milo finished and stepped back. Almost as an afterthought, he added, "Scripture says *soon*."

After rehearsal, Tad came to find them. "Hey, you two. Neil ran into Derrick in the foyer, and they're talking shop. If you want to head home now, you'd better catch a ride with Grandpa and Grandma."

"I'd rather stay," Prissie replied.

Tad nodded. "I figured as much, and that's fine. Neil may be a while. Wake me up when you're all ready?"

Prissie had to smile. Her big-big brother was just about the hardest working guy she knew, but he had a reputation of being lazy since he tended to fall asleep whenever he had some downtime. "I'll find you."

Koji nudged her. "May I greet the others?"

"Of course! That's why I wanted to stick around." A quick glance at the people milling below showed that both Baird and Kester were still up front. "Let's go."

Koji raced down the balcony stairs, bursting through one of the side doors into the sanctuary, but Prissie slowed down to admire the many stained glass windows. She could tell by the shadows drifting across the floodlights trained on them from outside that it was snowing again.

"Prissie!" She turned to see Baird jogging toward her. "Brace for impact!" he warned. Although she wasn't the sort of person who went in for public displays of affection, the exuberant redhead definitely *was*. Still, he pulled up just short and quietly asked, "Braced?"

"I guess," she mumbled, granting permission.

"Good, because you look like you need a hug," he asserted. Wrapping one arm around her shoulders, he gave her a quick squeeze, then herded her to the front where his teammates waited. "Rough day?" he asked lightly.

"It was," she admitted. "But after tonight, I'm feeling lots better."

"Glad to hear it!" Baird enthused before his expression grew more serious. "I'm *totally* available for hugs any time you need one, 'kay?"

"Thanks," she whispered, touched by the offer.

"Good evening, Prissie," Kester greeted.

Something about the way his dark eyes searched her face reminded her of Tamaes, and without thinking, she blurted, "I'm okay ... really!"

His eyes crinkled at the corners, and he inclined his head. "I am pleased to know it."

The last of the orchestra members drifted out the doors in the back, but Baird didn't seem in any hurry to leave. Instead, he gazed at the high ceilings and whistled sharply. Then he snapped his fingers, still eyeing the architecture. "Man, it's definitely built for music. C'mon, Kester, let's put this place through its paces!"

"There is the time to consider," Kester cautioned.

From over on one side of the room, an older gentleman called, "It's okay, boys. I'm the custodian, and I'll be busy for another hour or so. Knock yourselves out."

Baird bounded over, introduced himself, and shook the man's hand. "Thanks, Russ. You're a godsend!"

With a laugh, the man waved him away. "Enjoy!"

Racing back to the front, Baird propped his hands on his hips as he considered his options, then made a dive for the harpsichord. The score for *Messiah* was propped on the instrument's music stand, and as he riffled through the fat book, he called, "Kester, c'mere!"

His apprentice strolled over, saying, "Yes?"

"It's not every day we get to play with a harpsichord!"

"That is so," Kester agreed.

Patting the bench at his side, Baird said, "Sit, sit, sit!"

The tall angel unbuttoned his suit coat and dutifully slid onto the seat beside his mentor. "What did you have in mind?"

"Duet, duet, duet," he muttered, turning pages.

"You are speaking in threes," Kester pointed out, a trace of amusement underlying his tone.

Baird straightened. "Am I?"

"You are."

"Well, well, well! Maybe it just comes naturally?" The redheaded Worshiper struck a chord and warbled, "Holy, holy, holy ... !"

Koji tiptoed forward and peered over the redhead's shoulder, and Prissie followed. The young Observer inquired, "Are you going to sing?"

"Aha!" Baird exclaimed, thumping a page near the back of the score. "We don't sing all the songs during our performance, but there are some awesome ones in here. Which part do you want, Kester?"

"You may lead. I will follow."

Hopping to his feet, the redhead strolled around the harpsichord to face his partner, and Kester centered himself on the bench, running his fingers up and down the keys to get a feel for the instrument. Then he lifted dark eyes expectantly to Baird, who dimpled. "On three?"

Kester's lips quirked, and his long fingers plucked a few notes from the harpsichord. Almost immediately, Baird launched into a ringing solo. "O Death, O Death, where ... where is thy sting?"

The line repeated, but the second time through, Kester's baritone rose up. "O Grave, O Grave, where ... where is thy victory?"

To Prissie, it sounded as if the two Worshipers were singing different songs, but the notes wove together and occasionally meshed. It was like a game of tag, with the two melody lines chasing after each other. All too soon, it was over. Disappointed, she peeped at the music and complained, "It's so short!"

"Again?" Baird offered. Prissie nodded hopefully, and he twirled his finger at Kester. "Reprise!"

This time, she was able to follow the weaving melodies better, which only added to her appreciation. "Amazing," she whispered when the pair brought the song to its triumphant conclusion.

Immediately, the redhead leaned over the top of the piano-like instrument and wheedled, "Since I spoke in threes, let's sing in threes?"

"Switch parts?" Kester suggested.

"Now you're talkin'!" Baird agreed, rubbing his hands together.

Before his apprentice could resume, a deep chuckle rang through the sanctuary. "A musical taunt for the enemy?" Harken called.

"I'm feeling sassy," Baird replied, shoving his hands into his pockets with a sheepish air.

Harken's grin broadened as he took a seat. "By all means!"

As the third rendition of their duet wove its way into Prissie's heart, she followed Koji down the stairs and into the pew next to Harken. "Good evening," she whispered to the shopkeeper.

"It has been," he returned, patting her shoulder.

After the two Worshipers finished their threefold excerpt of Handel, Kester closed the harpsichord and waited while Baird wandered the platform, singing under his breath. The lights along the sides of the sanctuary started to flick off, leaving only the front of the sanctuary lit, and the redhead raised a hand at the janitor. Russ waved back and went on with his duties, leaving them to their fun.

Baird stopped his meandering, closed his eyes, and lifted his voice. There was no accompaniment this time, and his melody rose right to the ceiling, filling the sanctuary. Kester was soon humming along, and Baird beckoned for his apprentice to join him at center stage.

"What language are they singing in?" Prissie whispered.

Harken's smile was nostalgic. "Hebrew. Would you like a translation?"

"Yes, please." She scooted closer to the Messenger.

Harken shared the lyrics in a low voice. "It is good to sing praises to our God; for it is pleasant, and praise is beautiful."

As she watched Baird and Kester, Prissie couldn't have agreed more.

"He counts the number of the stars; He calls them all by name," Harken continued.

"He does?" she murmured, startled by the notion.

"Indeed," breathed Koji.

"He gives snow like wool. He scatters the frost like ashes. He casts out His hail like morsels. Who can stand before His cold?"

Prissie glanced toward the windows. It seemed an appropriate song to sing in winter, and as it drew to a close, she said, "The words were pretty. Did Baird write this one?"

"No," the shopkeeper replied with a small smile. "That was the 147th psalm."

"Oh," she murmured, embarrassed for not recognizing the passage. "So ... where's Milo?"

"He had some matters to attend to," Harken replied offhandedly.

“Something dangerous?”

“No more than usual.”

Worried in spite of Harken’s calm, she pressed for more. “Are Taweel and Omri with him?”

“Yes, Prissie.” With a steady gaze, he added, “Have faith.”

9

THE TREE GARDEN

Taweel stood at a point where the path split two ways and glanced uncertainly at his companion, whose raiment gleamed dimly in the utter darkness of the tunnel. "This way," Milo said, taking the right turning.

"Are you certain?" the Guardian inquired gruffly.

"I've never had a problem finding my way to a recipient," the Messenger assured. "When I am Sent, the way becomes clear."

"Same here."

Several minutes later, Milo sighed and pushed his hand through his hair. "I'd mind the darkness less if I could pass through it more quickly. Is Omri okay?" At the sound of his name, the little yahavim zipped forward, circling the Messenger twice before returning to his perch on Taweel's shoulder. Chuckling softly, Milo said, "I'll take that as a *yes*."

Nearly an hour passed before the narrow tunnel brought

them to a precipitous ledge. The path curved off to the right along the edge of the cavernous chamber, leading up to the heavily chained stone square that blocked the entrance to the Deep.

"*Finally*!" Milo breathed. Spreading his arms wide, he fell face forward into the chasm.

Taweel watched without comment as his companion dropped out of view, and a few heartbeats later, a blaze of blue light exploded past, climbing in exuberant loops toward the roof of the chamber before banking into a tight spiral back down. With a swift flick of his wings, Milo rejoined his teammate. "Feel better?" Taweel inquired, sounding amused.

"Much."

Together, they trekked up the wide path to the grinning Protectors flanking the gate. "Not used to the dark?" inquired one in a friendly way.

"Nope," Milo admitted honestly. "The close quarters were making me restless."

The second cherubim nodded understandingly. "What brings you to the Deep? Few Messengers are Sent where their voices can reach."

Raking his finger through long curls, Milo replied, "One of my teammates has been lost in darkness for a long time. I suppose I wanted to see for myself what he has endured."

Exchanging a quick glance, the first Protector spoke up. "Ephron?"

"Yes!"

His companion wiggled his fingers coaxingly in Omri's direction, softly remarking, "Your hair is the wrong color, but you must be just as brave as the one we seek."

"You know about Lavi?" Milo asked, glancing excitedly at Taweel.

"Of course," the guard replied seriously. "Thanks to Tamaes, I doubt there is a single angel in shouting distance who has not heard about the Observer who was taken ... and the stray yahavim who knows how to find him."

The other Protector said, "We all watch for signs ... and hope to be Sent."

Milo pressed his hand to his heart, murmuring, "I, too."

Even kneeling on her windowseat, Prissie had to stretch to reach the series of hooks screwed into the sloping ceiling overhead. With great care, she slipped a ribbon loop over one, suspending a precious Christmas ornament in front of the window. Sitting back, she admired the swaying treasure, a whimsical glass confection Aunt Ida had sent from Italy.

Koji sat cross-legged on her floor, quietly watching her fuss with the arrangement of her collection. The night before, they'd pulled names out of a hat for the family gift exchange. Prissie had *hoped* to pull the young Observer's, but instead she'd drawn Tad. From many years of experience, she knew her big-big brother was tough to shop for. Most years, his siblings got him practical gifts like gloves or slippers. She wondered if she could do better. Glancing at Koji, she casually inquired, "So who did you get?"

"Get?" he echoed, not following her train of thought for once.

"Your secret Santa name."

"I understood that the results of the drawing were

intended to remain a secret," the young angel replied, a trace of rebuke in his tones.

"Well, *yes*, but you could tell me," she coaxed.

"Then it would not be a secret," he gravely replied.

He had a point. "Well, I'm not going to tell you mine, either."

"I would not ask it of you."

"Of course you wouldn't, but I'm just stating it for the record."

Koji's dark eyes took on a shine. "Thank you for your consideration."

"Are you teasing me?" she grumbled.

"Indeed," he replied with a small smile.

Prissie shook her head in exasperation. Angels had the oddest sense of humor. Either that, or Koji was spending too much time with Tad. With a thoughtful hum, she reached for the next ornament in the box she'd brought down from the attic. Maybe she should look for an *im*practical gift for Tad this year, something he would appreciate because of who he was instead of because of what it could do.

"Your family's tradition is different than your class's tradition," Koji ventured. "I am unsure of the purpose of the elephant gifts."

"*White* elephant," Prissie corrected. "And they don't really *have* a purpose, except maybe to be silly."

"I do not understand."

"They're not *real* presents," she explained. "I mean, we'll wrap the gifts and everything, but they won't be anything nice. We give things no one needs."

The concept seemed to boggle the angel's mind. "I do not understand."

Prissie shrugged. "All the presents go on a table, and when it's your turn, you choose one. There's usually some kind of game that gives you the option to steal someone else's present. After a few rounds of stealing and swapping, that's it. You're stuck with whatever you're stuck with."

"What motive would you have to steal a useless gift?"

"It's not really stealing," she said in exasperation. "It's just a silly, old-fashioned game that the teachers always seem to choose! For instance, last year, Ransom really hammed it up. He opened a frilly shower cap, the kind with polka dots and a ruffle around the edge. Even though it made him look ridiculous, he claimed that it was just what he'd always wanted. No one had the heart to take it from him, and he ended up wearing it all day long."

"Why?"

"For the fun of it?" Prissie replied dubiously. "He's never serious about anything. At least, he wasn't back then."

"So it is possible to enjoy gifts that are pointless in nature."

"Yes, I suppose that's true."

Koji's expression cleared. "Then elephant gifts *do* serve a purpose. They allow you to enjoy the company of your classmates."

"I guess." She sighed. "The best white elephant presents are either mysterious, funny, or embarrassing."

"I will endeavor to amuse my classmates," he promised.

Prissie frowned. "You'd better let me be in on this one, just to be safe. Your sense of humor is very ... angelic."

With a mildly surprised expression, he replied, "Thank you."

The tractor clattered to a stop, and Prissie's older brothers jumped down in order to set a short set of stairs into place. They usually used this trailer for hayrides during harvest-time, but today, Grandpa Pete had pulled most of their family clear out to the back forty in order to choose this year's Christmas tree. Only Grandma Nell and Grammie Esme had stayed back to make sure there was coffee and cocoa ready when they returned. "Ready to strap on the old tennis rackets?" Grandpa Carl asked, giving his footgear a playful swing.

Jude giggled. "That's a *snowshoe,* Grandpa!"

Prissie stepped into her own snowshoes and listened in on more of her grandfather's trademark balderdash. "Few know it, but I was a lumberjack in my youth!" he boasted.

"For real?"

"Would I kid you, kiddo?" the old man countered. "Why else do you think I have flannel pajamas?"

Her youngest brother puzzled that out. "'Cuz they're warm?"

Prissie giggled softly, then glanced at Tad, who was waiting on Jude. Playing up to his audience, Grandpa Carl confided, "I was famous back in the day ... had a pet ox, to boot!"

"Named Babe?" Tad asked blandly.

"You see?" Grandpa Carl said triumphantly. "Your brother remembers!"

"You named your ox after a pig?" the six-year-old asked in disbelief.

Momentarily flummoxed, their grandfather rallied by asking, "Are you telling tall tales, Jude? Next, you'll be saying we're here to chop down a cherry tree!"

"No, a *pine* tree!"

Prissie shook her head and turned to Koji, who'd been

strapped into snowshoes by Beau. "If you walk normally, you'll trip yourself," her almost-twin explained. He demonstrated the proper stance. "Keep your feet shoulder-width apart, and you'll be okay."

The Observer stood and took a few cautious steps. "I understand. I appreciate your assistance."

"Yep," Beau acknowledged, tromping off after Grandpa Pete and their dad, who already had a head start toward the far hill.

Waving Koji over, Prissie pointed at a gentle slope about a quarter mile to the west of the newly-plowed road they'd followed back into the orchard. "We're going over there. It's the tree garden."

Pete Pomeroy had been growing the family's Christmas trees since the farm had been passed to him by his father. Prissie's dad had been small, money was tight, and Grandpa Pete thought it foolish to pay for something you could grow yourself. He regularly added to the stand of mixed evergreens by transplanting stray seedlings onto the roughly triangular slope leading up to one of their property's tree-lined boundaries.

The air was crisp, and the sky was clear as they crunched over drifted snow. Everyone was laughing and talking at once, so Prissie figured it was safe to ask, "Are we okay?"

Koji replied, "This is much easier than ice skating."

"Not that," she said in exasperation. Nodding in the direction of the fairgrounds and the ridge beyond, she muttered, "You guys said that we're close to trouble here."

He gazed around with a neutral expression, then quietly stated, "Fear not."

Prissie didn't find his gentle evasion terribly comforting.

"How is a tree selected?" Koji inquired.

"Height, shape, the number of branches for hanging ornaments," she listed. "Anyone can suggest their favorite, but Momma has the final say on which tree comes back with us. Once she makes up her mind, she'll tie her scarf onto one of its branches, and that's that."

"I see."

Once they reached the pines, the tree-hunters scattered, and Prissie eagerly lost herself in the evergreen maze. The trees had been planted in a zigzag pattern, so she meandered among them, letting her mittened hand brush over compact needles. Grandpa kept the trees neatly sheared, so each one had excellent potential. Choosing was usually difficult.

Out of the corner of her eye, Prissie caught the flutter of fabric and turned to see who'd followed her, but no one was there. Frowning slightly, she glanced around at the tracks in the snow. At least two other people in snowshoes had come this way before her. She could hear Koji's voice just beyond the next row of trees, where he seemed to be talking with Zeke. The eight-year-old was only too pleased to show their newbie the ropes. With a smile and shake of her head, Prissie began her own search for the perfect tree.

The sharp scent of pine filled the air because Grandpa Pete had already begun nipping boughs to make wreaths for their front doors. Closing her eyes, Prissie took a deep breath, releasing it with a sigh; when she opened them, she once again caught a flicker of movement out of the corner of her eye. "Who ... ?" she muttered to herself. Jedrick had assured her that the Hedge had secured their home, but did that mean just the house, all of the barns, or the entire orchard? Maybe it was time for her to find Koji.

Executing a neat turn in spite of her snowshoes, Prissie aimed in the general direction of Zeke's voice, but before she made much headway, a deep shout sent her heart into her throat. Green light burst into a set of widespread wings as Jedrick exploded into view, sword drawn as he dropped out of the sky. Automatically ducking, Prissie crept closer to a nearby spruce and peered past its branches. The Flight captain was engaging an opponent she could almost see. The occasional dark ripple that gave away its position never quite coalesced into a figure. Her desire to reconnect with Koji doubled, and she turned to call out to him, only to be confronted by an orange flare. "Tamaes too?" she whispered, truly frightened now.

Glancing around nervously, she couldn't decide which way to go. If she could see fighting on two sides, chances were unseen turmoil was on *all* sides. Edging as close to her sheltering pine as its prickles allowed, she kept her eyes firmly fixed on Tamaes. Her Guardian fought with a grim resolve that was fearsome to see.

Just then, Grandpa Carl and Jude tromped past, laughing and talking about pinecones, completely oblivious to the battle raging around them. The disparity wrenched at her soul, and she almost wished she were blind to the truth.

A sweeping blow from Tamaes's gleaming sword appeared to be enough to dispatch or drive off his opponent, for he turned then to check on her. Prissie waved from her hiding place, and his expression softened into a smile just before his gaze sharpened, and he scanned the area alertly. "Koji!" he called, his voice carrying across the tree garden. Moments later, the young Observer scuffed through the pines on his snowshoes. "Stay with Prissie," Tamaes commanded.

"I will!"

With a curt nod, the Guardian took off in Jedrick's direction, and Prissie gratefully locked arms with Koji, whispering, "What's happening?"

"A few Fallen appeared shortly after we arrived," he explained. "Jedrick was nearby, so he is lending his strength to the Hedge."

"Nearby?" she furtively echoed. "Why would a Protector be hanging out in the back forty?"

Koji hesitated before explaining, "Jedrick's responsibilities keep him close. We should not linger."

"But we can't *leave*!" she exclaimed. "My family's here!"

"I only meant that we should rejoin them," he assured.

Knowing that her brothers would be running back and forth to Momma, it made the most sense to get to her. "Is that way good?" she asked, pointing to where she could hear the sound of her mother's voice.

"Yes."

They moved together, but unfortunately, snowshoes were *not* made for closeness. Koji's became tangled with hers, sending them both tumbling into the snow.

"Allow me," offered an all-too-familiar voice.

Prissie's head jerked up, and she stared in shock into Adin's handsome face. He stood tall and proud, dressed in a neatly tailored suit and draped in a luxurious black cloak. "Quickly," he urged, holding out his gloved hand with a serene smile.

She felt the color drain from her face, for this time, she clearly saw something that had been invisible every other time she'd spoken with him. Adin's dashing appearance was spoiled by the set of ruined wings rising above his shoulders. They twitched and rustled, betraying his impatience, and with every shift, they rattled together in an off-key cacophony. Dull, lifeless shards, like grimy glass and clouded mirrors, hung from a twisted framework that had probably once been gracefully draped in light. "Your wings," she gasped.

For an instant, his expression hardened, but Adin rallied. "Never mind that. Come with me. I know someplace safe."

Scooting backward in the snow, Prissie choked out a weak, "No!"

Koji stepped between her and the looming demon, arms outspread. He'd slipped from his snowshoes, so he sank to his knees in the drifted snow. But his back was straight, and his voice was steady. "Do *not* listen to him, Prissie."

Adin's wings creaked as he lifted them higher, and Prissie panicked. She remembered what Koji had told her. Observers were ill-equipped to defend themselves. Scrambling to her feet, she grabbed her best friend around the shoulders and pulled him backward, dragging him out of reach of those wicked-looking appendages. When she fumbled to a stop, Koji turned in order to wrap his arms around her waist, and she clung to him desperately. He may have been the only thing keeping her upright.

Slowly, their enemy's face changed, twisting with a cruel smile. "Found me out, have you? Pity." His eyes darted skyward for an instant, then he touched his fingertips to his lips and blew her a kiss. "Until next time, Prissie Pomeroy!"

An instant later, he flickered out, vanishing completely as Tamaes's boots thudded to the ground right in front of them. The tree garden disappeared in a swirl of ticklish light as her Guardian's wings swathed them in sweet safety, and Prissie heaved a shuddering breath. "Just in time," she whispered, practically throttling Koji. "I was so afraid he'd hurt you!"

"I was frightened," he confessed in a soft voice.

"You were brave," Tamaes said as his wings parted so he could study his teammate and his charge. "Thank you for protecting each other until I could reach you."

Prissie wasn't sure if his hand trembled with fear or rage, but his touch was light as a feather when he briefly placed his hand atop her head, then Koji's.

"We are safe," the young Observer assured.

With an unhappy glance at the place where Adin had stood, she echoed their enemy's parting words. "Until next time."

10

THE HEAVENLY CHORUS

Raiment lent its soft glow to the otherwise pitch cavern where six Protectors stood watch over the formidable threshold to the Deep. The guards shifted restlessly, and one of the cherubim finally drew his sword. Other blades, a spear, and a bow were swiftly readied as eyes and ears picked up hints of a danger most grave—clicking of teeth, scuffing of feet, and a scrabbling like so many insects. "They come," whispered the bowman, his eyes fixed on the dark depths. "Stand firm."

Suddenly, light bloomed behind them, and they turned in surprise as a door opened from nowhere. Padgett's gaze swept their faces, then darted past them, taking in the oncoming tide. "I was Sent," he announced briskly. "Come away."

"But ... the Deep?" protested one of the guards, confusion plain on his rugged face.

"Leave it in the hands of God," the Caretaker said, holding out his hand. "Accept the mercy He is extending."

All six immediately strode past Padgett into the light, just as the first of the hoard surmounted the cliff. "A Caretaker," the demon hissed, eyeing him warily.

"Once a Protector. Now, a destroyer," the angel returned evenly.

"Get in our way, and you'll suffer!"

Padgett gazed passively at the Fallen who feared his presence. "I have already accomplished what I came to do."

The Fallen exchanged glances, and snickers rippled through the mob. "His hands are tied!" taunted one voice.

"Forward!" bellowed another.

A trollish demon bared decayed teeth in a gleeful grimace before lofting a wicked ax and bringing it down against the heavy chains that held fast the Deep. Sparks flew as the weapon skidded off the dark metal. "Not the chains, fool!" shrieked a voice from amidst the mob. "Strike the stone! Loose the anchors!"

The apprentice Caretaker quietly stepped back, taking every trace of light with him as he closed his door upon deeds best left to the darkness.

Prissie's family arrived early at Holy Trinity Presbyterian in order to secure good seats, for even though they'd doubled the number of Pomeroys on the stage this year, they still needed pew space for nine. The *Messiah* performance was probably West Edinton's most formal occasion each year, and

Prissie loved to see what people were wearing. They always brought out their finest—sparkles and sequins, fringes and fur, cashmere and cufflinks.

She was feeling rather fine herself. All of her friends had long-since given up new dresses for Christmas and Easter, but it was a tradition she clung to with Grandma Nell's help. This year's dress was cut from deep blue fabric with plenty of swish to it, and Prissie adored the way it swirled just above her ankles when she walked. The high waist was trimmed with wide, white satin ribbon that she'd chosen because it reminded her a little of the shining raiment she'd worn in dreams. And Momma had taken the time to weave Prissie's hair into a braided coronet that was almost like a halo, then added several hairpins decorated with tiny, pearly flowers.

Koji looked respectable in his new shirt and tie, and Momma had encouraged him to leave his long hair down. Prissie kept stealing glances, for with his black hair framing his face, he looked more like the angel she'd first met in the orchard. He noticed her stare and whispered, "Is this acceptable?"

"Very," she said firmly. "Even your tie is knotted correctly."

He touched the silk accessory. "Your father helped me."

"You look quite dashing."

Tucking his hair behind his ear, he leaned close to whisper, "I like these shoes. They do not have laces!"

Prissie knew he'd been excited about his new loafers when he'd polished them no less than three times the evening before, and she thought it was sweet.

Just then, Koji's gaze swung toward the orchestra section in front of the stage where the dark-clad musicians were already seated. The soft flutter of pages accompanied the low hum of conversation in the sanctuary. Following the young Observer's gaze, she spotted a latecomer working his way around to one of the empty stools on the side where the band members were set up. It took several moments for her to realize that the person picking up Baird's blue guitar was ... Baird.

The Worshiper's wild red hair had been smoothed back, and he wore a dark sport coat and tie. While he propped his hip on a tall stool and adjusted the strap of his guitar, Koji whispered, "Does he look quite dashing?"

For the first time in her life, Prissie found herself wishing someone would dress down instead of up. Frowning somewhat, she admitted, "He looks quite uncomfortable."

"Indeed."

The choir began filing onto the stage, and Prissie eagerly watched for her friends and family members. Soloists had special seats, and she was thrilled right down to her toes when Milo sought her gaze and smiled. After some orchestral tuning, the director strode to center stage, and when the applause faded, the music began.

Joyous songs lifted her heart to new heights, and she was sure she'd never experienced anything so grand in all her life. Having Koji close, she could hear him humming from time to time. Momma's smile was serene, and Prissie could just see her father tapping his toe in time to the music while he kept Zeke anchored to his side. "Is this like heaven?" she whispered.

The young angel solemnly replied, "It is a foretaste."

Afterward, Prissie wanted to run up with Koji to compliment Milo, but Grandpa Carl tapped their heads, saying, " ... and you, and you. In line, fussbudget. It's family portrait time!"

As Grammie Esme hustled them over to a spot in front of a glittering Christmas tree, Koji tentatively asked, "Me too?"

"Sure, sure, you're part of the family this year," Mr. Pomeroy said with authority. "We wouldn't dream of leaving you out!"

Koji's expression filled with wonder, and he murmured soft thanks before hastening to Prissie's side. She wasn't sure if he was simply touched to be included or if he wanted to see what he looked like in a photograph. It was hard to say with Koji because he didn't think about things in the same way she did. One thing was clear, though. He was happy. The young angel stood as close as possible, holding tightly to her hand and beaming while the shutter snapped over and over.

When Grandpa Carl declared himself satisfied, Prissie eased her hand out of Koji's and waved for him to follow. Once they were out of her family's earshot, she asked, "What's put you in such a good mood?"

"Your family has made me most welcome," he replied. "And I am glad there will be a record of my place at your side."

It was an odd way to refer to a photograph, but Prissie shrugged it off when she spotted Kester, who sat quietly in the orchestra section. He looked perfectly natural in his dark suit, but the way his long fingers drummed against the surface of his cello betrayed some measure of restlessness. "You're still here!" she greeted, glancing around. "Are you the only one?"

The tall angel gazed up at her with solemn eyes. "I believe so. Baird asked me to stay here."

She smiled a little. "Did he mean *here* in the church or *here* in your chair?"

"He did not specify," Kester replied with chagrin. "Did you enjoy the performance?"

"Very much," she enthusiastically assured. "It was wonderful, but ..."

His gaze remained locked on hers as he quietly inquired, "Is something on your mind?"

She fidgeted. "Is something the matter?"

"Why do you ask?"

Peering around the emptying sanctuary, she replied, "Harken and Milo disappeared almost as soon as the concert ended. It's not like them not to visit with their friends and neighbors."

He inclined his head, saying, "They had messages to carry."

"I guess that *is* what they do," she said hesitantly.

"That is so."

Prissie still had an oddly off-kilter feeling. "And, if you don't mind my saying so, you seem less calm than usual. Are you worried about them?" she probed.

Kester exchanged a speaking glance with Koji, then said, "I care deeply about my teammates. There are times when it is difficult to stay behind and wait."

"Is this one of those times?" she asked nervously.

Small crinkles at the corners of his eyes accompanied a humorless smile. "Most assuredly."

Koji shook her shoulder and whispered, "Prissie, please wake up."

"Hmm?" she murmured into her pillow, then lifted her head, squinting at him in the darkness. "Koji? What's wrong?"

"Shield your eyes," he quietly urged. "I am going to turn on your lamp."

With a soft grumble, she slapped her hand over her eyes, and she heard the soft *click*. Even though her bedside lamp wasn't very bright, it took several moments to adjust. "Koji," she complained, glaring at her clock. "Please tell me why you woke me up at three in the morning. You might not need sleep, but I...."

"I apologize," he whispered. "But they are coming."

"What?" she asked. "Who?"

Koji simply pointed to the ceiling, which had begun to ripple. In a rush of green light, Jedrick dropped into the room and glanced her way. "Do not be afraid, Prissie," he said before turning his attention back to the ceiling. "Or perhaps I should have said, 'Do not be angry'?"

Flustered by the sudden arrival of the Flight captain in her bedroom, Prissie shook her head. "I'm not mad. Not *really*," she admitted. "Just confused."

Suddenly, another huge warrior dropped through her ceiling, and she squeaked in surprise. This angel's skin was dark as night, a striking contrast to his iridescent wings, and he had twin swords strapped to his back. Glancing her way, he smiled faintly. "Fear not, Prissie."

Though she couldn't imagine why, there was something familiar about this angel, and she tentatively asked, "Have we met?"

"In dreams," he replied simply.

"Who ... ?"

"My name is Lucan, and that is enough for now."

"But ... !"

Lucan held a finger to his lips. "Hush, little daughter. Your own Guardian is our main concern at the moment."

Prissie gripped her quilt with white knuckles. "Tamaes?" she whispered, glancing fearfully at Koji.

The young Observer touched her arm comfortingly. "He is stubborn."

Meanwhile, Lucan and Jedrick moved into position, and Jedrick quietly called, "We are ready, Taweel. Lower him through."

A pair of boots dangled into view, followed by long legs, and the two waiting angels reached up to brace the limp form supported by Taweel's strong arms. The big Guardian leaned right through the ceiling and waited until Lucan said, "We have him," before relinquishing his hold on Tamaes. Withdrawing momentarily, Taweel re-entered the room feet first, and suddenly, Prissie's tiny bedroom was jam-packed. She huddled closer to Koji, who wrapped his arm around her shoulders.

"Is he ... ?" she choked out.

"Mending," Taweel quickly assured, holding out his arms and reclaiming his sagging apprentice.

Jedrick turned and knelt beside Prissie's bed. "Earlier this evening, the Deep was breached."

"Isn't that place full of demons?"

"Yes, and the moment the chains were ripped from the stone, those Fallen boiled up out of the pit," said the Protector. "When the enemy finds a toehold, a crack, a weakness, there is a rush to exploit it. Many fled into the tunnels, and many more scattered across the surrounding countryside. Because your family's farm is nearby ..." With a grim shake of his head, Jedrick explained, "The Hedge was unequal to the onslaught because most of your Guardians followed your family into town for the concert."

Prissie's gaze swung from Taweel to Lucan, then back to Jedrick. "There are demons here?"

"They *were,*" the captain clarified. "By the time everyone returned, many of the Fallen were already entrenched, but with the help of each Guardian's Flight, we have reestablished a boundary."

"That's been hours now!" she gasped.

"True," Jedrick replied. "And the struggle is far from ended."

Taweel assessed the small space her bedroom offered, then sat in the same spot Tamaes had chosen the week before. With great care, he and Lucan arranged the unconscious Guardian so that he leaned back against his mentor's chest. Tamaes's head lolled to one side, and he looked strangely bare without any armor covering his raiment.

"How was he hurt?" Prissie asked, eyeing the shimmering bandages swathing his shoulder and neck.

"An enemy's arrow." Rolling his eyes upward, Taweel gruffly said, "You can let go now."

Omri raised his head and peered out from amidst the big Guardian's thicket of black hair. With a blink, the yahavim took in his surroundings and immediately flew to Lucan. Hovering for a moment in front of the silver-eyed warrior, he suddenly swooped through a series of somersaults. Light intensified around the little yahavim, and a large wafer of manna drifted onto Lucan's waiting palm. With a deep chuckle, the warrior said, "Thank you, sweetling. The refreshment is most welcome."

The little angel flew to Jedrick next, repeating the process. The captain gravely said, "Thank you, Omri."

Next, the tiny manna-maker zipped to Koji, landing on

his shoulder and patting his cheek. The Observer whispered, "I am well, but Prissie is too pale."

Omri hopped over to her shoulder and gently petted her cheek, as well. "I'd feel better if you helped Tamaes for me," Prissie confided shakily.

With a flurry of wings, the yahavim launched himself at the injured Guardian. Producing another wafer of manna, Omri landed on Tamaes's chest, creeping up until he could press the food between his lips.

"Are the other injured in the barn?" Koji asked.

Jedrick nodded. "Tamaes was billeted there, but Abner finally begged us to ferry him over here. In his determination to reach Prissie, Tamaes was making a nuisance of himself."

"Not steady on his wings at the moment," Lucan remarked. "I caught him crawling across the yard."

Tamaes stirred and groaned, "Prissie."

Taweel's hold tightened on his apprentice. "She is here, safe and sound."

Lashes fluttered until reddish-brown eyes opened enough to search her out, and Prissie lifted her hand. "Here I am."

Tamaes's gaze wandered to the others in the room, then he reached up to grasp his mentor's arm. "All safe?" he asked.

Taweel grunted softly, and Tamaes took it as an affirmative. "May God be thanked," he murmured, and with a sigh, he sagged back into unconsciousness.

Jedrick shook his head. "The arrowhead was poisoned. He needs time."

"I will remain here," Taweel declared.

"So be it," Jedrick replied simply. "Padgett will check on him later."

Nodding curtly to Prissie, Jedrick leapt up through the

ceiling with a short flick of shimmering wings. Taweel leaned forward, giving himself a little room, and awkwardly extended his wings in the confined space. With a soft tutting, Lucan lent him a hand so the Guardian wouldn't bump anything off Prissie's bedside table. She watched in awe as he lifted them up, out, then forward, carefully draping their soft folds over Tamaes. Lucan briefly fussed at the edges before murmuring, "I will be on the roof. Rest easy." Then, in a flash of pearly white light, he whooshed upward and disappeared from view.

The room felt big and empty without the looming warriors, and when Koji jumped off the bed to hurry to Taweel's side, Prissie followed. "Is there anything I can do?" she whispered as she knelt on the braided rug.

Taweel shook his head. "Normally, our activities do not disturb our charges. Please, forgive the intrusion."

"Don't be silly! I want you here if it means you'll be safe!"

His lips quirked, and he pointed out, "Your safety is *our* charge, little one."

"Yours?" she asked in surprise. His thick brows drew together, and she clarified, "I thought it was your job to watch over Milo."

"Tamaes is my apprentice. If he cannot be by your side, I will be."

"Oh, I didn't realize!" she exclaimed softly. "So in a way, you're mine too!"

"In a way."

She stared pensively into this second Guardian's scarred face, noticing anew the faint lines that criss-crossed Taweel's dusky skin. Tipping her head to catch his bashful gaze, she said, "Thank you."

"Back to bed. You will only worry him if you catch cold."

Prissie obediently returned to her place, snapping off the light before wriggling down under her covers, but Koji climbed onto her windowseat. He lay at an angle across its cushions, gazing down at his injured teammate. After a time, he dangled one hand, wiggling his fingers in a silent plea for Tamaes's attention, but the warrior was too far gone to respond. Instead, Taweel lifted one big hand and clasped Koji's in a gentle expression of shared concern.

Their closeness made Prissie feel a little lonely, but with a flutter of wings, Omri flew over. He landed with a soft plop on her quilt and skipped lightly to her pillow. A smile crept onto her face as the yahavim blinked at her with faceted eyes that glittered darkly against his luminous skin. "You're like a tiny drop of sunshine, aren't you?" she murmured.

He hummed, then clambered up onto her pillow and curled up where he could watch her.

"I haven't needed a nightlight since I was little," she said. "But I think tonight I want one, and you'll do nicely."

Omri's response was a funny little series of hums and clicks that made her look to Taweel for a translation. Both he and Koji were watching her with bemused expressions. "What?" she asked self-consciously.

The big warrior shook his head. "He is scolding you, little one."

Her face fell, but Koji interjected, "I have only ever heard Omri scold Taweel. I believe it means he likes you."

"He *has* taken to you," the Guardian agreed.

Prissie gazed at the glowing sprite as Koji quietly explained, "A yahavim always knows what is needed."

"And what do I need?"

Omri hummed insistently, and Taweel huffed. "You and Tamaes both need rest."

"Oh," Prissie breathed, carefully nestling down beside her tiny companion. She was sure it would take a miracle for her to get back to sleep after so much excitement, but miracles seemed so much more possible when you shared your pillow with a wee bit of heaven. Within minutes, she found her way into peaceful dreams.

11

THE CLASS PARTY

"Heavy chains slow his progress, but as you can imagine, he is difficult to pin down," the cherubim reported. "Do you remember him?"

"You bet," Baird replied, glancing up from his messages. "Shimron should too."

"I have already conferred with him," Jedrick assured. "However, I wanted to check with you. You are somewhat removed from the situation, and that makes your perspective … unique."

The redhead paused in the process of texting and remarked, "If I had a nickel for every time I was called *unique*, I'd have a pocketful of change!"

"Myron," his captain sighed, using the Worshiper's first name.

Smile fading, Baird said, "Everyone's talking about the

whacked out weather up your way. Goes without saying that he's the one stirring things up."

"Agreed … though that is the least of our worries."

"The rest of the escapees?"

"They cannot hide for long."

Baird nodded. "Is Adin the one who planned that little jailbreak?"

"Undoubtedly."

"I'm guessing he didn't do it for kicks." Jedrick simply nodded, and the redhead drummed his fingers on the side of his phone. "The enemy doesn't *need* a reason to create havoc, but Adin's different than most. What's he after?"

Jedrick spread his hands wide, begging ignorance. "Shimron believes their sole goal may have been the release of this one demon."

Baird shook his head. "The Fallen don't help each other; they *use* each other. Freeing that big fella was hardly charity on Adin's part, which means there's *another* goal."

"Agreed."

"Given everything else that's gone down, I think you should warn the one in the most danger."

"Prissie?"

The redhead's brows shot up. "Seriously?"

"We have been Sent to support Tamaes," Jedrick pointed out, green eyes intent.

"No doubt!" Baird agreed. "And she totally needs looking after, 'cause the fallout's gonna be a doozy, but I doubt Adin is turning heaven and earth upside down for her sake."

The Protector's expression grew thoughtful, then grave. "Your words ring true, which means …"

Baird's gaze drifted northward as he finished his captain's hanging thought. "Adin's probably looking for Aril."

By the middle of the next week, Grandpa and Grandma Olsen finished packing and provisioning their RV, and the whole family was up extra early to see them off before school. "We must take flight before this weather gets any more serious," Grandpa Carl declared, dramatically tossing the end of his scarf over his shoulder. "The reports say you'll be kicking up more winter in these parts. If we stay any longer, we'll be drifted in 'til spring!"

"Smootchies!" Grammie Esme demanded, starting the rounds of goodbyes. She went around the room twice—once for hugs, once for kisses—before announcing, "We left a little something for your stockings with your Momma, so think of us at Christmas!"

The chorus of promises and porch-side waving continued until their big rig rumbled out of view, bound for the highway and points south. It all left Prissie feeling a little wistful, but she was startled to notice tears in Koji's eyes. "What's the matter?" she asked in concern.

"I have discovered that I do not like goodbyes," he confided softly.

"Nobody does," she retorted.

"Unless it's to someone you're glad to shake loose," interjected Neil, who clapped the Observer's shoulder on his way back to the kitchen, clearly aiming for a second helping of breakfast. "Then it's good riddance!"

Curious, Prissie asked, "Who would *you* want to get away from?"

Her older brother shrugged. "Pests."

"There's always one," Prissie's homeroom teacher muttered as she added a glitzy package to the pile of gifts on the table in the back of the classroom. Everyone had been instructed to wrap their white elephant gifts in either newspaper or plain brown paper, but the latest contribution arrived in gaudy green-and-red wrappings. It stood out from the crowd, and Prissie felt sorry for it. She could sympathize.

Most of her classmates had opted for casual attire since they only had a half-day before being released for winter break, but she'd kept with tradition and wore her Christmas dress. She felt uneasy with her decision because everyone seemed to think she was trying to draw attention to herself. Some of the ruder comments stunned her, but they also made her furious. No one made fun of Elise for dying her hair or Marcus for always wearing his leather jacket. Why was a nice dress worse ... or even something worth teasing about?

"Where'd you get *that*?" Elise demanded in disdainful tones.

"My grandmother made it," she replied curtly.

"It's homemade?" her classmate asked, looking her up and down. "How *weird*. You people even make your own clothes."

Prissie had no words for the spiteful girl, so she cast a hopeless look at Koji, who'd joined her by wearing his shirt and tie. She appreciated the moral support, but it was small comfort. He simply wasn't drawing the same unwelcome attention, and she envied him his providential ability to fade into the background. Keeping her head high, she strode to her seat.

Just then, Ransom ambled into the room and remarked in passing, "I don't remember that one."

She stiffened, waiting for some sly follow-up, but the teen just dropped into his seat and turned to Marcus. How odd. He hadn't paid her a compliment, but he'd noticed her dress. Ransom's opinion meant *nothing* to her, but it still made her happy that he'd been not-rude. Cheeks flaming, Prissie turned in her seat and fixed him with a surly glare.

He did a double-take and quirked a brow. "What's up?"

"Thank you," she muttered, turning her back again.

His silence was followed by a low murmur of voices that Prissie did her best to tune out. Right as the bell was ringing, Ransom tapped her shoulder, and whispered, "Say, Miss Priss."

She turned her head just enough to hiss, "What?"

"Marcus wants me to tell you that he thinks so too."

"Thinks *what* too?"

Ransom blinked abashedly. "Well, crap. He got me."

Prissie frowned at the Protector slouched in the desk kitty-corner behind hers, but Marcus didn't react.

"Well, fine. Whatever," Ransom grumbled. "You look nice, so don't listen to the ones who say otherwise."

For the second time in the space of two minutes, Prissie found herself at a loss for words. The world was probably ending. Yes, that was the only possible explanation for the bane of her existence to turn out to be considerate.

As usual, Prissie's party contribution included two big boxes of cupcakes from her father's bakery, and they were welcomed with enthusiasm, especially by the boys. To her relief, Ransom never brought up the fact that he'd handled the icing. He only ate them one after another, grinning over the teasing he received. "Best cakes in town come from Mr. Pomeroy's place!" he boasted.

"He's like a walking billboard for Loafing Around," she complained to Koji.

The young Observer nodded thoughtfully. "He is not ashamed."

In addition to the baked goods, there were chips and pretzels and two-liter bottles of soft drinks. The health nuts in their class were satisfied with a veggie tray and a bushel basket of apples from the Pomeroy's orchard. April and a couple other girls set up a coffee bar in the corner, which turned out to be the most popular of all the refreshments.

"Oh. Em. Gee! Could this be more boring?" drawled Elise, earning a chorus of snickers. She shot a look in Prissie's direction with a smirk that spelled trouble.

Prissie sighed and wondered why the pouting girl hadn't skipped school.

No matter what Elise or the other students said, Prissie liked the gift exchange part of the proceedings. It was fun and funny to see what everyone had brought. When April opened her package, she turned her gift over and around, clearly mystified. "What *is* this thing?" she asked.

Prissie authoritatively announced, "It's a ricer. You press boiled potatoes through it."

Her friend fiddled with the handle and asked, "Why?"

"Obviously, to get rid of lumps," she explained. "Or if you serve potatoes riced, they have a pretty texture."

"It looks more like a giant play dough toy!" someone heckled.

"Everyone knows mashed potatoes come from a box!" another kid offered.

Prissie shook her head at their ignorance. It wasn't as if the ricer was *that* unusual. Grandma Nell used theirs all the time! When Prissie's turn came, she rescued the poor, misunderstood implement, giving April the chance to try for another mystery package.

Some of the prank gifts were awful, and others were awfully funny. Silly trinkets. Broken oddments. Unwanted clutter. Ransom whooped with laughter when Marcus opened a box that contained a pink mug with *Daddy's Little Princess* printed on the side. The whole class yowled when Ransom turned around and opened a lumpy package containing a battered fedora. He donned the hat, tilting it at a rakish angle and defying anyone to try to take it from him.

Prissie was honestly enjoying herself until one of her classmates opened the gaudy little attention-getting package and lifted out a turquoise blue diamond of glass, framed by translucent marbles in shades of blue and green.

Koji's hand reached out, but she snatched hers away before he made contact. There was no way she was letting Elise see her clinging to him for comfort. Head high, she did her best to tune out her classmates' comments as the noisy game continued, for many were vying for the pretty sun-catcher. No one wanted the ricer she cradled in her lap, so it was safe. But the gift Prissie had given Margery for her birthday at the end of summer was quickly passed from one pair of hands to the next.

Prissie stole a peek at her former best friend, but Margery was whispering with Elise. Jennifer looked as if Christmas had come early, but April's face was pinched with concern.

She met Prissie's gaze squarely and whispered, "There must be some mistake."

Koji and Marcus traded a long look, and then the Protector leaned close to Ransom and said something that lifted his eyebrows. Prissie doubted she could take any further embarrassment, so she slipped from her chair, quietly excusing herself to the refreshment table. She caught her teacher's eye, pointed at the door, and mouthed a request for the bathroom. The last thing she saw before making her escape was Elise's smug smile.

Maybe she was selfish. Maybe she'd been naïve. Either way, Prissie had hoped that Elise was just another of her old friend's many fads. Margery was supposed to come around, see the error of her ways, and apologize so that everything could go back to the way it had been. But for the first time in her life, Prissie realized that *wanting* something wasn't going to change anything.

Somehow, she pulled herself together enough to return to the classroom and endure the time that remained before they were bussed home. On her way out, Marcus called, "Prissie, wait!"

She couldn't disobey the Protector, especially since Koji grabbed her hand and dug in his heels, preventing her from bolting. With a weary sigh, she faced Marcus. "What?"

He held out a clumsy bundle of tissue. "This is important to you."

Just enough colored glass stuck out at the edges for her to know what his offering contained. "Who says?" she demanded, keeping her hands at her sides.

"April explained." Marcus lowered his voice. "She wanted you to know that Margery doesn't know how this ended up in the exchange."

Prissie felt sick. She hadn't even rated an apology, just a third-hand excuse. "You're a Messenger now?" she asked sarcastically.

"Seems like," he replied with a shrug. "Take it."

With an injured look, she whispered, "I don't want it either. You keep it."

Marcus hesitated, then nodded. "I'll keep it safe for you," he promised as he tucked it into his pocket.

"Funny how the weather down here isn't half so bad as ours," Beau remarked.

"How much snow didja get?" asked one of his youth group buddies.

"Our place is drifted under."

"Whoa, lucky!"

Beau protested, "Not when you're the one trying to keep the walkways clear!"

Prissie hid her smile under her scarf. Poor Beau. Unlike the rest of her brothers, he really didn't care for the out-of-doors. He dragged his feet whenever chores took him away from his books or computer.

The latest storm seemed to have stalled right over West Edinton, and the boys had been shoveling since sunup. A little ways away, Tad yawned hugely. Prissie had half-expected him to beg off of the Wednesday night service, but he'd insisted that he wanted to take part in the caroling beforehand. She wondered if he *really* wanted to be here, or if he just hadn't wanted to disappoint Koji. Tad could be thoughtful like that.

"I wish to greet Kester," Koji whispered, giving her a hopeful look.

"Go ahead. I'll be right here when you get back."

"Indeed. I will return shortly."

He darted toward the tall Worshiper, who was stationed off to one side of the group, and she automatically searched for Kester's mentor. Baird might be a little flighty, but he turned out to be pretty good at herding cats. Prissie supposed that part of it was that this was the third caroling go-around, so most of the youth already knew the routine, but there was no denying that the Worshiper could hold a crowd's attention. This evening, the redhead wore a ridiculous, rainbow-striped hat with a huge yellow pom-pom on top, so even though he was shorter than more than half the crew, he was easy to spot. "Just follow the bouncing ball," she murmured wryly.

"Yeah ... bouncy," agreed a voice just behind her shoulder.

Glancing back, she did a double-take. "What are *you* doing here?"

"I'm not even sure, to be honest," Ransom replied in an undertone. "Your brother invited me."

"Which one?" she asked, mystified.

"Neil."

"And you're humoring him because ... ?"

"Curiosity, mostly," he admitted. "Your dad talks this place up, and that band was pretty good when they played in your barn."

"Oh," she replied. "So ... do you sing?"

"Not very well," he admitted with a shrug. "You?"

"Not very well," she grudgingly confessed.

"Then what are *you* doing here?" Ransom asked, turning the question around on her.

Prissie frowned thoughtfully; there were a lot of possible

reasons. Practically speaking, her older brothers had wanted to go caroling, and they were her ride. Also, while Koji hadn't said anything *specifically*, she knew he was eager to take part, and he would never have come without her. But mostly, she'd wanted to hear her angelic friends sing. Baird, Kester, Milo, and Koji were all present and accounted for, and their harmonies lifted her heart like nothing else. Giving her braids a toss, she declared, "I guess because it sounded fun."

"Go figure," Ransom replied with a smirk. Glancing around, he said, "If this turns out to be any kind of fun, I might try to drag Marcus along next week. Maybe some of the other guys."

"Really?"

"Why not? I don't think Joey sings, but I know Brock is pretty good. He'd probably come just for the cocoa."

Fleetingly, Prissie wondered what had happened to Koji. He could have rescued her from carrying on a conversation with Ransom ... not that it was so bad. With a jolt, she remembered that Ransom probably didn't know anyone except her and her family. A small smile crept onto her face as she remembered one of her father's favorite sayings: *"Knowing the Pomeroys is like knowing half the crowd."*

Just then, an exuberant redhead sidled up to them, cheerfully greeting, "Miss Pomeroy! Mr. Pavlos! Glad you could make it!"

"Hello, Baird," Prissie replied, shaking her head at his whimsical formality.

"How would you like to join our rhythm section tonight?" Looking both ways, he leaned closer. "Kester totally refused these, but it'd be a shame if they went to waste!"

"Jingle bells?" she asked, picking up a set and giving it a gentle shake.

"Yup!" he exulted, pushing the second set onto Ransom. "You can ring-ting-tingle all over the place! It'll be all *seasonal*!"

"*Now* I remember!" Ransom blurted, shaking a finger at the redhead. "I *remember* you!"

"From that day in the barn?" Baird ventured. "Beau Pomeroy's birthday gig?"

"Before that," the teen replied. "You were in the alley behind the bakery on Halloween!"

"You're right, I was," the Worshiper replied, suddenly serious. "You saw me?"

"Kinda hard to miss, with those glow-in-the-dark pajamas," Ransom replied. "What were you supposed to be in that get-up?"

"What did I look like?"

"Radioactive."

The redhead broke into a huge grin. "I like that!"

"Really, though ... how did you put out so much light?" Ransom asked curiously.

Laying a finger beside his nose and winking, Baird replied, "Trade secret."

Prissie had already resigned herself to the fact that Ransom would probably be sitting with her family during the service. Her folks arrived, and her dad was all smiles to find his part-timer mingling with his lot. During the scramble for seats in the gymnasium, Prissie filed in from one end of the row Tad had reserved only to meet Ransom in the middle. She turned around to march right back out, only to run up against her father.

"Trade?" she begged.

He firmly replied, "Sit."

Her pained expression was still in place when she slunk into her seat, but Ransom was too busy talking with Neil on his other side to notice. Leaning forward, she looked for her usual companion only to spot Koji sitting with Milo on the end of the row ahead. Twisting the end of her braid around her finger, she wished she was sitting with them instead. Ransom was too close for comfort.

As if to confirm this, the teen bumped her with his elbow. "I have *no* idea what I'm supposed to do," he confided in a low voice.

"You've never been to church before?"

Ransom shook his head. "I had to go to a wedding once, but I don't think that counts."

Prissie shrugged. "Just do what everyone else does."

"I'd rather know *why* everyone else does what they do."

"Well, this isn't exactly my church," she explained. "We do things differently than they do here."

Her classmate's eyebrows quirked. "So you don't do what they do? Huh. Do you think they're doing it wrong?"

Feeling a little defensive, Prissie replied, "No, I just don't do everything they do because they do some things I don't want to do."

"I thought you said I should do what everyone else does," he challenged. "Strange advice from someone who doesn't!"

This was getting ridiculous. With a stern look, she demanded, "Are you doing this on purpose?"

"Doing what?" he asked innocently.

Prissie flapped her hands in exasperation. "This!"

"Yep. Totally on purpose."

Rolling her eyes, she muttered, "I'm done."

His brown eyes were shining. "It was fun while it lasted. But seriously, though ... I might have questions."

"Why me?" Prissie folded her arms. "You could ask Neil."

The music started, and the only answer she received was a shrug and a crooked smile. Something told her it was no use. Ransom was determined to pick *her* brain ... or maybe just plain pick on her.

He behaved all through the first part of the service, standing and sitting at all the right times. It made sense that he didn't know any of the songs, but he wasn't rude about it. As far as Prissie could tell, Ransom mostly gazed with curiosity around the gymnasium while drumming his fingers against the side of his leg. Then Pastor Kern jogged to center stage and launched into a brief recap of his Christmas series.

Almost immediately, Ransom leaned over and asked, "Is he serious? 'Naughty or Nice'?"

Prissie frowned at him. It wasn't polite to talk during service.

"Don't give me that look. I warned you I'd be asking questions," he whispered back.

"Just *listen*. He'll explain himself better than I could."

Ransom tilted his head to one side, then nodded, conceding the point.

Dennis Kern was saying, "Naughty and nice, good and bad—they sound cut and dried, but there are times when everything isn't as it seems."

Stealing a peek at her angelic friends, Prissie nodded to herself. It was true. Appearances could be deceiving.

"Take reputations," the pastor continued. "There are those who have *good* ones; they're respectable citizens with all the appearances of righteousness. We have a prime example right here in the Christmas story—Herod! This king in his castle greets the wise men from the east, telling them he wants to worship the child of prophecy, the same as them. Herod says all the right things, but there's murder in his heart."

Ransom muttered, "Yeah, I read about him. He was bad news."

Prissie shivered and whispered back, "I don't like lies ... or liars."

"On the other hand, you have someone like Mary, the young woman chosen by God to give birth to His Son. She did *nothing* for which she should be ashamed. Nowadays, Christians consider the role she humbly accepted to be an honor, calling her *favored* by God. But was she praised for her choice at the time? Her family, her friends, her fiancé—they all believed that she'd sinned. Scandal nearly cost her upcoming marriage, and although the rumors and speculations were unjust, I'm sure they hurt. The poor girl's reputation was shot."

"Relate much?" Ransom whispered. "They're giving you crap at school, but it's a farce."

"I haven't done anything wrong," Prissie muttered.

Jostling her again, he pointedly replied, "Me, either, but *some* people can't be reasonable."

"There's another reputation to consider in the Christmas story!" Pastor Kern exclaimed, scanning the congregation. "The good and the bad are easy to peg, but have you ever considered those with *no* reputation? They were right there, in the thick of things, the rabble of the hillsides—lowly men with humble livelihoods. No one expected anything from a bunch of men who watched over the herds. No fame, no status, no skills, no expectations—yet these were the ones to see the sky fill with angels, to hear the heavenly chorus, to learn the good news!"

Ransom poked her arm. "Is that where you put me?"

Prissie was a little surprised by his question, because she'd been thinking that maybe this was where *she* fit into the story. It was awfully easy to relate to a group of ordinary shepherds who were minding their own business, only to have their world turned upside down by a bunch of angels. She happened to glance Milo's way, and the Messenger held her gaze and nodded once. "Yes?" she murmured uncertainly.

"Rabble," he mused sarcastically. "Nice to know where I stand."

Desperately hoping her father hadn't overheard, Prissie held up a finger to hush Ransom, just in time for the pastor to declare, "Those with no reputation are in good company, since Paul tells us that Jesus made Himself of no reputation. That very night, when He was born, Jesus became nothing ... but also everything we need!"

Bible pages riffled as the congregation turned to Philippians, and Ransom sat a little taller. From that moment on, his smart-mouthed comments ceased. He was locked in with startling intensity to what Pastor Kern had to say. Prissie should have been relieved that he was finally leaving her alone, but maybe she was spoiled by the usual constancy of Koji's company. Yes, that could explain why she was once more feeling lonely in the middle of a crowd.

12

THE SHOPPING FRENZY

"Good morning, Milo."

The deep voice flowed soft and slow, a warm rumble of sound that could startle the unprepared, but the Messenger's ready smile widened in greeting. "Same to you, Aril."

"You are early."

"My wings were restless. And I didn't think you'd mind if I turned up before sunrise."

Aril waved a large hand to the stone step on which he sat. "Your company is always welcome. Come aside and tell me your news."

"Little has changed," Milo admitted. "Most of my days are filled with ordinary things."

"I do not mind," Aril assured, but his orange eyes studied

the Messenger thoughtfully. "Though I am curious about your confession."

The Messenger's brows lifted. "What did I say?"

With a note of amusement, Aril replied, "Restless wings are rarely a sign of peace."

"I suppose not," Milo conceded, running his fingers through his hair. Then, he blinked and murmured, "What if ... ?"

"Yes?"

"Instead of speaking of ordinary things, what if I told you an *extraordinary* story ... about a girl whose eyes have been opened to heavenly things?"

Interest piqued, Aril answered, "Tell me."

Prissie was disappointed with progress. Despite her best intentions, she wasn't getting very far with finding presents for the people she counted dearest. According to Momma, Christmas presents were an expression of love, not an obligation. She always told them that small things, even intangible things, could be more thoughtful than any of the stuff money could buy.

The more Prissie wandered through the stores in West Edinton, the more she was forced to agree with her mother. Shelf after shelf was stocked with merchandise, but nothing struck her as appropriate for any of her angel friends. "How do you shop for an angel?" she groused.

Koji shook his head. "I do not know. I have never tried."

With a frustrated huff, she begged, "Do you see *anything* here that might work?" Dark eyes darted from shelf to bin, and Prissie could practically see him dismissing it all. "No good?" she asked with a dreary sigh.

He shook his head, but remarked, "One never knows what God can use. Even if I do not understand the purpose of a thing, that does not mean it has none."

"I give up," she grumbled, heading for the door. "Let's go." She pulled her hat around her ears before stepping outside. The wind had whipped up so much, it was hard to tell which way it was coming from. Snow whirled at them from every direction, and she pulled her scarf up over her nose. "We'd better hurry. It's gotten worse."

"Indeed," Koji agreed, squinting against the icy gusts.

Prissie struck out, aiming for the bakery, but a sudden noise froze her in her tracks. The deep groan rose to a high, angry screech that made her want to cover her ears. Looking over her shoulder, she tried to place the sound but came up empty. "What was that?"

"You heard?" Koji asked, eyes wide.

"Obviously," she scoffed, peering through her lashes toward the sound's origin. "Maybe someone's roof was pulled loose by the storm?"

The noise ripped along the vacant street again, harsh and off-key, and this time, Prissie saw something moving against the dizzying whiteness. Koji grabbed hold of her arm so quickly, she nearly dropped her bag. "No!" he shouted. "No, that is not what it was!"

"What *is* that?" she asked, her voice shaking. Though the figure was indistinct, she could tell that the dark shape moving toward them was taller than most of the buildings on Main Street.

"We need to go!" Koji said sharply.

Prissie nodded nervously. "Yes, I think we should go. The bakery, or Harken's?"

As the pair glanced uncertainly up and down the street, poised to make a run for it, Prissie caught sight of a familiar figure shuffling along on the other side of the street. The scene took on a nightmarish quality as Ransom headed straight for the hulking shadow that loomed larger by the moment.

A tree branch creaked and cracked, plunging to the snow-covered lawn in front of the town hall, narrowly missing the gazebo. Ransom turned to look at the sudden noise, and Prissie's heart leapt to her throat. She might not like the guy, but she couldn't stand by and do nothing. Things had changed.

Koji pulled on her arm again, but she shook it free and raised mittened hands to her mouth. "Ransom!" Her voice came out shrill and faint against the wind, so she took a deep breath and bellowed his name again.

This time, he spun to face them, and she waved desperately for him to come over. "This way! Quick!"

To her relief, Ransom changed direction and ambled their way. "What's up, Miss Priss?"

"It's not safe! Come with us!"

He glanced around with a bemused expression. "It's just snow."

Prissie latched onto his arm and cast a fearful look at the shadow. Panic thrilled through her soul. "Which way, Koji?" she begged.

The young Observer quickly grabbed Ransom's other arm and gravely said, "Please, come this way. It is a matter of some urgency."

"If you say so," Ransom relented. "Geez!"

They ran all the way to Harken's, bursting through the door in a tinkle of chimes. While Koji firmly closed the door behind them, Prissie puffed, trying to catch her breath. Still clamped onto Ransom's arm, she carefully enunciated, "Good evening, Mr. Mercer. Sorry to barge in so late, but it's getting bad outside. Can we wait in here?"

Harken's smile was reassuringly familiar. "Of course, Prissie! Won't you introduce your friend?"

At a sudden loss for words, she looked blankly into her companion's face and quickly let go of his arm. He quirked an eyebrow before speaking up for himself. "Ransom Pavlos, sir. Mr. Pomeroy has mentioned you some. I work at his bakery."

"Jayce's apprentice!" Harken exclaimed, smiling broadly. "It's a pleasure to make your acquaintance! Make yourselves comfortable," he urged. "Prissie, you should call your father to let him know you and Koji are here. We don't want him to worry."

"Yes, please. Thank you." She hurried through to the back room and placed the call, then returned to announce, "Dad says if it's okay with you, we should stay put. He and Uncle Lou have the chess board out, and they're making do over at the bakery. The boys will come dig us out tomorrow."

"You're most welcome," Harken assured. "Are you expecting a ride, Ransom?"

"Nope. I walked."

"I see," the old shopkeeper murmured. "Would you like to place a call to your parents?"

"Sure, yeah. I'll let my dad know where I am," he agreed.

Just then, Milo strolled through the back room's door and said, "We've got a blizzard on our hands!"

"Hey, Mr. Mailman," Ransom greeted.

"The name's Milo," he reminded with a chuckle.

Ransom grinned. "I remember. Which way to the phone?"

"Through here," he said with a courteous sweep of one arm. "It's on the corner of Harken's desk."

"Gotcha."

While her classmate put through his call, the Messengers compared notes. Harken said, "I've conferred with Jedrick. Half a legion is mobilizing, but they cannot fight a storm."

Milo heaved a deep sigh. "Abner says he hasn't been Sent. There's nothing he can do."

Prissie wandered over to where Koji stood looking out the window. She could barely see the streetlight on the corner, let alone the bakery. A pickup truck edged past at a crawl, snow up to its hubcaps, but it was soon lost from view. "How bad is it?" she whispered.

"I do not know," he replied honestly. "However, we are safe here."

"What about Dad and the others?"

A series of loud pops startled her, and she looked up and down the street. "There," Koji offered, pointing at sparks arcing into the air from a transformer. Just like that, the power went out. The lights and furnace stalled simultaneously, plunging the bookstore into eerie silence.

"Hang on," Milo ordered. "I know where to find some light. Everyone sit tight."

A clatter and thud of falling books came from the back room, and Harken called, "Ransom?"

"Sorry, sir. I bumped into something-or-other."

"Are you hurt?"

"Nah, I'm fine," the teen assured.

They lapsed into silence while they waited for Milo to reappear, and Prissie's eyes strained for some trace of light. The blackness was so complete, it reminded her of being lost in the tunnels that had led her to the Deep. Shivering, she mumbled, "It's too dark."

"Indeed," Koji quietly agreed.

Prissie was disappointed when he didn't reach for her hand. More than anything else, she didn't want to feel alone, so she reached for him, her fingers finding the rough cloth of his coat sleeve. "Can you see?" she whispered.

"The storm has blotted out the stars, but even so, I can distinguish more than you are able."

Tugging on his sleeve, she edged closer to her friend. The scene on the street haunted her memories, and she couldn't seem to stop trembling. "I think I'm scared," she admitted.

"We are safe," Koji repeated. After a short pause, he announced, "Milo is returning, and he is not alone."

In the next moment, light shimmered from the direction of Harken's office, and Prissie gasped. She could clearly see Ransom's profile now; he leaned against the wall, hands in pockets, head down, and he didn't react at all when a flood of tiny angels streamed past him, bringing their brightness into the room. He was blind, but she could see.

Only when the beam of a flashlight cut through the dark did Ransom react, turning toward the sound of Milo's cheerful hail. "I found what we need! Hey, Ransom, did you get through to your family before we were cut off?"

"Yeah," he replied, accepting a spare flashlight and clicking it on. "I told Dad I was hanging out with you guys until the storm calms down. He didn't care."

"I see," Harken replied gently, taking a box of candles off Milo's hands. "I'm sure you put his mind at ease."

Ransom shrugged and looked at Prissie. Holding up the flashlight, he asked, "You want this?"

"N-no," she stammered, trying very hard to act naturally. Abner's entire flock seemed to have escaped into the bookstore, and their antics were more than enough to make her forget her fears. Many of the manna-makers danced acrobatically through the air, while still more explored the odds and ends Harken had on display. The little dears were so distracting!

Oblivious to the small angels whirling just over his head, Ransom quirked a brow at her. "What are you smiling about?"

"I'm just glad there's light," she fudged.

"Afraid of the dark?" he guessed, cautiously working his way across the room.

"Not usually."

"'Cause you can have this if you are," he insisted.

She meant to glare, but a pair of yahavim got between her and him. With a warm smile, she replied, "No, thank you. I don't need it."

"Huh." He moved to the front window. "Well, I'm glad you yanked me off the street when you did." Using his hand to shield his eyes as he peered through the glass, he casually added, "Though I still don't understand *why* you did."

Koji said, "Prissie was concerned for your safety."

"Uh-huh," Ransom replied dubiously, squinting down Main Street. The whole building rattled as a gust of wind ripped past. "Do you think they're okay over there?"

"I'm sure they're safe, but they can't be very comfortable," Milo said as he emerged again from the back. He dropped a pile of blankets on the counter and gazed thoughtfully at the teen. "How about this? We'll add some pillows to this pile, and you and I can tote them over to the bakery. We'll camp out with them tonight."

"I'm okay with that," Ransom agreed.

"I'll bring down the pillows," Harken offered. "Ransom, would you mind lending me a hand?"

"Happy to, sir."

As soon as they were out of earshot, Prissie hurried over to Milo. "Isn't it too dangerous to go out there?" she asked worriedly.

"I'll do what I must, Miss Priscilla," he answered seriously.

Koji helpfully supplied, "He has been Sent."

"Oh." With an unhappy little sigh, she whispered, "Be careful."

"We will," Milo promised.

Once Milo and Ransom were bundled out the door with their bulging packs, Harken locked up and waved Prissie and Koji toward the back room. "Let's wait in the glade," he suggested. "Prissie, see how many of the yahavim you can get to follow you. Koji, keep a sharp eye out for dawdlers. Abner won't thank us if we misplace any of his little ones."

It didn't take long to coax the tiny angels through the blue door. Prissie did her best to tally them up just to be sure, but it was even harder than counting chickens. "I can't even guess if they're all there!" she admitted in exasperation.

"Abner will manage it," Harken assured with a chuckle. "He calls them by name."

"Tamaes!" greeted Koji, trotting over to the Guardian.

Prissie studied the tall warrior closely, checking for bandages. "Are you all better?"

"I am well," he replied, gesturing to the soft grass. "Take your ease so we can talk."

"About what?" she asked.

"Forces are gathering," Harken said solemnly. "I could try to give our news a positive spin. Of all those who escaped from the Deep, only one eluded our search."

"One demon can't do much ... right?" she asked uneasily. Looking from face to face, she asserted, "If it's just one, it's not a big deal."

Tamaes and Harken exchanged a long look, and the Messenger sighed. "Let me see if I can explain. Having met us, I think you'll understand the gravity of our situation."

"Okay?" she prompted.

"I'm a Messenger. Tamaes is a Guardian. Koji's an Observer. Malakim, hadarim, adahim—we're all Faithful."

Prissie knew this much, so she nodded. "Orders of angels."

Harken continued, "Before they Fell, the enemy were as we are. They once served God as Messengers, Guardians, Protectors, and so on."

When he paused again, she said, "That makes sense."

"A few ... a *very* few of the fallen were Caretakers."

That had an ominous sound to it, and Prissie asked, "Is that a problem?"

With a nod, Harken explained, "Caretakers were given great power, surpassing that of all the heavenly host."

Tamaes chimed in, reciting, "Star-movers, earth-shakers, sea-stirrers, storm-bringers."

Harken added, "Caretakers tend the heavens and earth at God's command. Not one of them acts on their own initiative."

Prissie thought she understood. "But an enemy doesn't listen to God anymore?" she asked in a small voice.

"Indeed," Koji replied solemnly.

"Does that mean … ?"

Tamaes confirmed, "The one who eluded recapture was a Caretaker."

"He's a disaster waiting to happen," Harken said. He waved a hand to indicate the darkened shop and blizzard on the other side of the blue door. "It has already begun."

13

THE LIVING NATIVITY

Dinge and Murque traded jabs, each trying to force the other to voice the question on both their minds. Their scuffling standoff grew tiresome, so with a faint sneer, Adin sweetly inquired, "Something to say?"

Clearing his throat, Dinge asked, "Why her, my lord?"

"Are you questioning my taste in prey?"

"There's easier pickings," Murque pointed out.

"She's cozy with that whole Flight," Dinge added peevishly. "They crowd around her like a misbegotten Hedge!"

"Let them fret and flutter," Adin replied dismissively. "The girl's only a means to my ends."

"Isn't that what you said about the Observer we snatched?" Murque grumbled. At his superior's narrow glance, he hastily added, "No offense, my lord. I just don't see what you're aiming for. If it's not the apprentice … and it's not the girl … then, what?"

With a superior sniff, Adin announced, "I hear interesting things."

"Do tell, my lord," Dinge coaxed with a sly smile.

"That Tower, for instance."

"There's plenty of towers," Murque remarked.

"True," Adin conceded, his eyes glittering. "But this one *moves*."

Prissie couldn't have been more frustrated, for a thousand little things seemed to be going wrong. Gum in her hair. Spiders in the bathtub. Missing library books. Her Saturday had ranged from one small catastrophe to another, and she was in no mood to smile by the time her father dropped them off at the door of First Baptist. She'd have to dredge one up, though. Tonight was their church's annual living nativity, and she and Tad would be reprising their roles as Mary and Joseph.

"Careful! There are still icy patches," called the shepherd who was scattering salt on the walks.

Prissie thanked him for the warning. "A sprained ankle would top off a day like today nicely," she whispered with a sour face.

Koji offered, "You may hold onto me."

"Says the angel who can't skate," she teased.

"Angel?" interjected Beau, who was walking right behind them. "Koji's a shepherd tonight."

"O-obviously," Prissie floundered. Really. Could the day get *any* worse?

It felt as if someone was out to get her, and stepping through the doors into the foyer only confirmed her suspicions. She was sure Milo would have called it some kind of providence, but she was convinced it was a divine conspiracy. With a hearty groan, she asked, "Not you too?"

Ransom exchanged a glance with Marcus, then shrugged. "You talking to me, Miss Priss?"

"Not tonight." Prissie shook her head and walked on by. She was too worn down by disasters to bicker with an annoyance.

"Blunt," Ransom said with a mock wince.

Marcus only grunted and fell into step behind her.

With a quirk of an eyebrow, Ransom followed suit, remarking, "Brave."

Koji laughed softly, and Prissie threw him a questioning look. "Ransom is good at seeing the heart of things," he whispered.

Two long tables in the foyer were arrayed with coffee makers and cookie platters for those who wanted to stop in for some fellowship. For the most part, however, the living nativity was a drive-by scene, and folks came from all around to inch past a makeshift stable set up in the corner of the parking lot. There were plenty of live animals, people in costume, and seasonal music.

All Prissie needed to do was dress warmly, hold a bundled-up doll, and spend a couple of hours in the spotlight. She was just heading over to get into her costume when Tad came jogging through the foyer. "Priss!" he called urgently.

She turned as her big-big brother slowed to a stop. "The sheep are loose, and they need my help to herd them back into the pen. Can you quick find a stand-in?" He was already jogging backward toward the entrance. "Sorry!"

"It's okay!" she replied, then sighed as she turned to Koji. "What next?"

"Stand-in?" Ransom asked curiously. "You have a part in the nativity?"

"Yes," she replied curtly, looking around for help, then waving urgently. "Momma!"

Mrs. Pomeroy hurried over and listened calmly to the explanation. "I see!" she said, her gaze sweeping the foyer. Almost immediately, she zeroed in on Marcus and Ransom. With a hopeful smile, she asked, "Gentlemen?"

Marcus cuffed his friend's shoulder. "He'll do it."

"No!" Prissie protested. She lifted pleading eyes to her mother's face. "Momma!"

"It's settled," Naomi said with finality.

Prissie knew better than to argue when her mother took that tone, so she said nothing more as Mrs. Pomeroy grabbed Ransom and Koji and hustled them to the changing rooms. Marcus watched them go, then fixed Prissie with a stern look. "Be nice," he growled.

"Why should I?" she countered peevishly.

"Because he's my friend."

That took her aback. She knew firsthand what it meant for an angel to claim a human friend. It was a rare thing, counted as precious, and her face fell. "Oh … right."

The Protector smiled. "Thanks, kiddo."

"Well, this is definitely not a role I ever planned on playing," Ransom said out of the corner of his mouth.

"It was nice of you to step in." Prissie replied with grim politeness. They could hear the whoops and hollers of those still trying to herd the sheep back toward the church. "I was really surprised to see you here."

"At church?" he replied, pausing to smile as flashbulbs went off from the window of a passing car.

"At *my* church."

"What's the big deal? Do I need a membership card or something?"

"Of course not," she grumbled, adjusting her grip on the swaddled bundle in the crook of her arm. "I was just really surprised to see you and Marcus."

"Your brother invited me," he explained, giving a small wave to the kids staring at them from the windows of a slow-rolling minivan.

"Which one?"

"Jude this time," he replied. "He said if I came, I'd get to see angels."

She gaped up at him. "What?"

"Oh, hey! There they come!" Ransom exclaimed, rolling his eyes at the robed figure making his way over. "Hey, Mr. Mailman! Are you Gabriel?"

"That's the general idea," Milo replied with a grin. Someone had sprayed golden glitter in his hair, and he wore a halo made from silver pipe cleaners; still, he maintained a certain dignity. "I heard you were pinch-hitting this evening. How does it feel to be in Joseph's shoes?"

"Awkward."

The Messenger chuckled. "Sounds about right, given all he was going through at the time."

Ransom said, "Guess so." With a wave, Milo moved on, and the teen frowned thoughtfully. "Huh."

Prissie peeked at him out of the corner of her eye. "What?"

He gazed into the starry sky overhead and remarked, "Crazy dreams, road trip, no vacancies, new baby who's someone else's, and a bunch of shepherds showing up in the middle of the night telling stories about an angel invasion." With a wry smile at the bundle in Prissie's arms, he muttered, "Talk about having your life turned upside down."

Prissie looked skyward as well and wondered how many invisible angels were winging overhead. "I think it must have been nice ... having angels promise them there was nothing to fear."

A car horn honked, and they turned in time to see Neil race past, his shepherd's robe flapping as he pursued a pair of bleating sheep. "Head them off!" he hollered to Tad, who was circling around from the other direction.

Ransom snickered. "I think I lucked out landing the Joseph schtick. Marcus and the rest of them are playing Little Bo Peep."

"How long have you and Marcus been friends?"

"About as long as you and me have been not-friends," he joked. Her lips thinned, and he answered more seriously. "A couple years ... going on three. I'd just moved here, and we were both new at the same time."

It was difficult to see anything past the spotlights trained on them, so she couldn't tell where Marcus was. If he was as good with sheep as he was with chickens, she supposed he was doing his part quite well. "Why are you friends?"

"Why?" he repeated, giving her an odd look. "Beats me. Just happened that way. How 'bout this, Miss Priss. Why are *we* not-friends?"

Another car full of kids rolled by, and they paused to smile for another series of camera flashes. Prissie scrambled for an answer but came up empty. As the vehicle moved on, she eyed him skeptically. "You want to be friends?"

"Dunno," he replied. "Maybe. Any reason we shouldn't be?"

She couldn't believe they were having this conversation. "Are you messing with me just because I can't get away?"

His eyebrows shot up, and then he grinned. "Gosh, Miss Priss! That's a good point. You're at my mercy."

"Figures," she muttered.

"I'm *kidding*," he sighed. "Just humor me and answer the question."

Prissie gave the baby doll in her arms a gentle pat and swayed as she tried to make sense of Ransom's demand. Finally, she tentatively admitted, "I don't like you."

"Yeah, you said so before, but I thought maybe that was changing." At her sullen look, he pointed out, "You and Koji pulled me inside that bookstore the other day. Very heroic. Almost friendly."

She was rescued from answering when a jeep paused in front of the nativity. Its window lowered, and a ringing voice declared, "Glory to God in the highest, And on earth peace, goodwill toward men!"

Prissie squinted against the lights. "A-abner?"

"Hey, Mr. Ranger!" Ransom said with a wave. "And ... other Mr. Ranger."

Padgett sat forward, a hand upraised in greeting. "Good evening."

Abner leaned even further out the jeep's window to gaze at the twinkling stars, "It *is* a good evening. Weather cleared up nicely, don't you think?"

"Yes, sir," his companion patiently agreed. "However, I was simply greeting Prissie and Ransom."

"As was I," the Caretaker retorted.

"Say, Abner!" Prissie dared to call, then ducked her head when she remembered they were in public. "I mean, Mr. Ochs?"

He peered at her over the top of his glasses, gray eyes patient and piercing. "Yes, Miss Pomeroy."

"Are you good with sheep? My brothers are having herding issues."

With a wintery smile, he replied, "As it happens, I do know a thing or two about straying flocks. Fear not, Prissie."

"Thank you!" she called as they moved along and turned into a vacant parking spot.

"Friends of the family?" Ransom murmured as they smiled for the next carload.

"Friends of *mine,* actually." She cringed the moment she realized what she'd said.

"Yours, huh?" He mulled that over for a while before saying, "I think you broke my brain."

"Excuse me?"

At that precise moment, the side door of a red minivan slid wide, briefly blasting them with strains of the *Nutcracker Suite,* and a familiar voice exclaimed, "Nice togs, Koji! Very ancient nomadic! But where's your flock?"

The young Observer, who was stationed just beyond the corner of the makeshift stable, gravely replied, "Abner will lead them back."

"Wagging their tails behind them?" Grinning ear-to-ear, Baird spread his arms wide. "Prissie! Ransom! You've got that whole re-enactment thing going on! Totally brings back memories! Right, Kester?"

"It is nostalgic," replied his apprentice, with a nod to each one present.

The other members of Baird's band waved and offered Christmas wishes before moving along, and this time it was impossible to ignore Ransom's hard look. "Friends of yours?"

"Obviously," she muttered, avoiding eye contact by attempting to burp her baby.

"What am I missing here?"

His amusement made her uncomfortable. "What do you mean?"

"When it comes to making friends, you draw from a pretty wide range of citizenry. Why am I disqualified?" She tossed her head, and he pressed, "Did I *really* blow it that big when I tied your braids together in the sixth grade?"

He was laughing, but his gaze was steady, and Prissie hated being put on the spot. She cast a longing look at Koji, but her good friend was clearly not Sent to her aid. On her own and out of options, she cut to the heart of the matter. "Habit."

Ransom's eyebrow quirked. "Really?"

She faced forward, trying to look like a serene mother instead of a flustered girl. "It's tradition," she said defensively. "That's the way it's always been."

"Habit," he reiterated, shaking his head in wonder. "And here I thought ... huh."

"What?"

"Smile for the camera!" he said through his teeth. She managed a lopsided smile, and he muttered, "Should I be amazed that Jesus still pulls in the paparazzi?"

"Don't make fun," she warned.

"Wouldn't dare," he assured.

After a few more cars passed by, Ransom gave her a nudge. "I was just thinking ... if you don't like me, but you don't know *why* you don't like me; doesn't it make sense that if you found something likeable about me, we could be friends? Hypothetically."

Her promise to Marcus about being nice weighed heavily on her mind. "I suppose that's possible. Remotely."

"A challenge!" he exulted.

"This is unbelievable. Doesn't *anything* embarrass you?"

"Not much," he admitted. "Why? Are you embarrassed?"

"Mortified."

"Why?" he asked, sounding genuinely curious.

"Because you're you, and I'm me," she replied. "And this whole conversation is ridiculous!"

"How about I tell you something embarrassing about me," he proposed.

"Like what?" she asked, curious in spite of herself.

"What if I told you my favorite color is pink?"

She blinked. "You're kidding."

Ransom gestured broadly. "Why would I lie about something so stupid?"

"Has anyone ever asked you your favorite color before?"

"Well, sure."

"And you told them *pink*?"

"Are *you* kidding?" he scoffed.

Dripping sarcasm, Prissie asked, "So you've lied to everyone except me?"

"What can I say? I'm turning over a new leaf."

"I'll believe it when I see it."

Ransom folded his arms over his chest. "Does that mean you'll be watching?"

"Watching my back," she returned tartly.

"In case I try to tie another knot in your hair?" he inquired, reaching behind her.

She shied away, and he relented as another car pulled into the church parking lot, illuminating a rather subdued flock of sheep trotting obediently to their pen. Neil slumped gratefully onto a straw bale beside Koji to catch his breath. “All woolies present and accounted for. Good thing Ranger Ochs showed up when he did. Him and the other guy did good.”

“Padgett,” Prissie supplied. “I hope you thanked them.”

“Several times,” he assured.

Tad sloped over and said, “Not sure who’s more worn out—us or them.”

“Coulda been worse,” Ransom offered. “Coulda been camels!”

Prissie’s older brother chuckled. “Want to trade places now that the excitement’s over?”

“I don’t mind sticking around.” Glancing at Prissie, Ransom added, “Unless *you* mind.”

“I don’t care,” she replied stiffly, once more conscious of being in the spotlight.

When the boys settled into their places as shepherds, Ransom leaned closer so that only she could hear him. “Will you keep my secret?”

“Your secret’s safe.”

“Does that make us friends?” he pressed.

“No.”

“Didn’t think so,” Ransom admitted. “But it’s a start.”

Prissie was afraid he might be right.

After the spotlights had been shut down and the farm animals loaded into their trailers, the Pomeroys warmed up inside the church with hot cider and cookies. Ransom and

Marcus stuck around ... and stuck close. "How'd you get here, anyhow?" Prissie thought to ask.

"Hitched a ride with Mr. Mailman," Ransom replied.

"You called?" Milo inquired, ambling over with a cup of coffee in hand. He'd shed his costume, but his hair still glinted in the lights. Noting Prissie's gaze, he gave his hair a pat. "How long do you think it'll take to get this stuff out?"

"You'll have metallic dandruff 'til Easter," said Neil.

"I could loan you a curry comb," offered Tad, his gray eyes sparkling.

Laughing at his own expense, the Messenger turned slightly as Mr. Pomeroy strolled over with the rest of the family. Right away, Prissie's father offered a hand to the young Protector. "We met once before ... Marcus, right?"

"Yes, sir," the teen replied with gruff politeness. "Marcus Truman."

"I hear you were pretty handy when it came to heading off those sheep," Jayce said. "Thanks for helping out in our time of need!"

"No big deal," he replied. Zeke stepped forward, staring hard at Marcus, who offered a cautious, "Yo."

"What happened to your hair?" the boy asked bluntly.

Marcus smirked and crouched down to let Zeke get a good look. "Nothing much. It's just hair."

"But it's different colors."

"And?" the Protector challenged.

Ransom snickered softly as Zeke continued his inspection, then turned to his mother to ask, "Can I have two, too?"

"Maybe when you're older," Momma replied, unperturbed by the boy's fascination. With Zeke, if it wasn't one thing, it was another.

"What colors do you like?" Marcus asked, his expression serious.

Zeke's expression scrunched thoughtfully. "Orange and red … like fire!"

"Hide the crayons," Ransom advised in an undertone.

"Are you kidding?" Prissie whispered back. "He moved beyond crayons when he was three. I'd say hide the spray paint."

"We could try food coloring," Ransom proposed.

Her eyes widened in alarm. "*Don't* give him any ideas!"

Koji raised a finger to his lips, enforcing her plea with a shush, and Ransom held up his hands in surrender.

As usual, the visiting went on long after the clean-up was done. Prissie sat on the floor next to the bench where Tad had sprawled and let her eyes slide shut. She was exhausted—both physically and emotionally—and all she really wanted right now was home and bed. Conversation melted into a pleasant buzz as she drifted perilously close to sleep, but as soon as she was quiet, the nagging sense of urgency returned. What was it she was forgetting? She could almost remember … almost….

"Miss Priss?" came a low voice. "You okay?"

She woke with a start and stared in confusion at Ransom. "Umm … what?"

Her classmate sat beside her before gesturing at her face. "Why are you crying?"

Touching her cheek, she found it wet and quickly scrubbed at it, muttering, "I can't remember."

"Bad dream?" he ventured.

She sniffed and shook her head. "No … I mean … there's something I've forgotten."

Ransom slouched against the wall. "You know something's missing, but you don't know what it is?"

"Yes."

"Let's see," he mused aloud. "Did you turn in all your homework?"

"Of course."

"Are all your farm jobs done?"

"Farm jobs?" she echoed incredulously.

"Sure. Milk the cows, slop the hogs, sheer the sheep—farm stuff."

She giggled in spite of herself. "We don't keep cows or sheep, and Tad and Koji are in charge of the pigs."

Ransom glanced at her sleeping brother and nodded. "If the porkers are covered, then maybe it's ... a birthday?"

"No," she sighed. "And it's useless to guess. I told you, I can't remember."

"But it's important, right?" he countered.

"I think so." Shaking her head, she admitted, "I *know* so."

"Maybe I'll jog your memory. Besides, it'll pass the time until Mr. Mailman has his fill of chit-chat."

Prissie looked around the foyer and soon spotted Milo, who was caught up in conversation. "That could be a while."

"No big deal. I get to sleep in tomorrow."

She frowned. "But tomorrow's Sun– Oh. Right."

His smile was a little sheepish. "Guess you'll be right back here in the morning."

"Yes."

Ransom stretched out his legs, then asked, "Is something lost?"

Something wasn't, but *someone* was, and Prissie winced. "Why do you ask?"

"Dunno. I guess there's not much difference between lost and forgotten," he explained. "Out of sight, out of mind."

"Oh," she managed, suddenly feeling uncomfortable. Was that it? Not quite.

She must have been lost in thought for a while because he reached over to tap her shoulder. "I think you drifted off with your eyes open."

"Sorry," she muttered.

His eyebrows slowly rose. "Can I borrow that frou-frou thing in your hair?"

Reaching back, she touched the satin ribbon she'd used to tie the end of her braid. "This?"

"Yep."

"Why?"

He held out his hand. "Because I know a remembering trick."

Baffled, Prissie gave one end of the ribbon a tug, then pulled it free and handed it over.

"Hold out your hand," he instructed.

To her amazement, Ransom proceeded to tie it around her finger in a big, floppy bow. "What's that supposed to do?"

"I hear it helps." Giving his handiwork a pleased look, he said, "Worth a try, right?"

"That's just silly!"

"No sillier than the other stuff you seem so willing to rely on," he defended.

"Like what?"

"Prayer," Ransom calmly replied. "Don't you think it sounds weird to believe that talking to someone you can't see will change things?"

"There are things we can't see," she retorted.

"How do you know if you haven't seen them?" he reasoned. "Do you pray?"

"Of course," Prissie huffed.

"And does it change things?"

"Things have changed," she replied moodily, refusing to meet his eyes.

"Well, then, Miss Priss," Ransom said, a challenge in his tone. "Maybe you should practice what you preach."

14

THE EARLY GIFT

Jedrick dipped toward Harken's store, but banked sharply when he realized that his apprentice was perched on a neighboring building. Spiraling lower, he landed lightly on the roof of West Edinton's newspaper office and strode over to Marcus. The younger angel had been especially preoccupied over the last few days, and the tension radiating from him was worrisome. "Why so downcast?" Jedrick asked lightly.

Marcus's drooping wings twitched up and out in belated defense, but quickly sagged again. Golden eyes glanced guiltily at Jedrick. "M'not."

"What then?" Jedrick inquired, taking a seat next to the youth.

"Can't you feel it?" Marcus asked in a low voice. A shiver rustled through his wings, and his gaze swerved back to the bakery across the street. "Something's about to happen."

Startled, the Flight captain scanned Main Street for signs of trouble. Despite the steady drift of snowflakes, the roads and sidewalks were busy, but the angelic contingent was unusually quiet. There was a heaviness to the hush, as if the unseen world held its breath in expectation. "I would not be surprised if there is another attack," Jedrick mused aloud.

"That's not what I meant," Marcus corrected. "This time, it's gonna be something good."

By midday on Christmas Eve, Loafing Around's shelves were cleared and the doors were locked. Only Jayce and Ransom remained to close down the bakery for the rest of the year. "Everyone and their uncle will be on a diet starting next week," Mr. Pomeroy announced prosaically. "So the key to our survival is healthy breads. We'll be running specials on all things whole grain and multi-grain ... or what my wife likes to call birdseed breads."

"Sounds rough."

"More like roughage!" quipped Jayce. "I'll mess with some gluten-free recipes at home just to see what's what, but we're usually right back in the cupcake business by Valentine's Day."

"Chocolate season?" Ransom asked.

"Sure, sure," his boss agreed. "We'll have a whole line of chocolate desserts in February."

Once he finished wiping down the ovens, the teen stretched. "Not sure what I'll do with a whole week off. Sleep I guess."

"It's good to take a break once in a while," Jayce declared. "This is my annual vacation. I like spending the week with my lot while they're off from school. It's a good way to end the year. Together."

"I get that. Sounds nice."

"Do you have plans with your family?" Mr. Pomeroy asked.

"I don't think you can call them *plans*," Ransom admitted carelessly. "My dad isn't much for celebrations, but this year, I thought I'd take over the cooking. It'll be better than ordering pizza." Jayce's expression didn't really change, but Ransom saw concern reflected in his blue eyes. Shaking his head, he said, "Don't worry about it, sir. We get by."

"What about your mother?"

"Not sure," he admitted. "She took off back when I was a kid, and she doesn't call."

Jayce sighed. "I see."

Ransom appreciated that. No false apologies, just acceptance of this newest tidbit of information.

"So it'll be the two of you?"

"That's right ... unless he works overtime." Ransom reached for the disinfectant as he explained, "Sometimes he grabs extra hours 'cause of the pay."

"I can understand that."

"We've never really made a big deal of the holidays, but this year's been pretty festive," Ransom shared. "I've been baking Christmas cookies all month. Went caroling. Shoot, I even played Joseph in that nativity deal." Pausing thoughtfully, he added, "It was fun and all, but this is also the first year I actually understand what all the fuss is about."

Jayce glanced over his shoulder. "I know you've read the Gospel accounts."

"Yeah. More than once," Ransom readily admitted. "I

finished the New Testament, reread some parts, and I'm making some headway in the Old Testament. It's sorta all fitting together."

"What are you going to do about all this new information?"

Ransom leaned against the counter and folded his arms over his chest. "Prissie says I know enough to make a decision."

Jayce straightened. "She said that?"

"Yeah. I sorta cornered her with some questions a few weeks ago, and that was her opinion."

"And what's your opinion on the matter?"

"She drives me crazy," Ransom muttered.

"Prissie does?" Mr. Pomeroy chuckled. "Why?"

"It's the strangest thing," he complained. "She's the absolute worst at explaining why she believes, but she's got the whole faith thing by the tail. Even if people are making fun of her, she's holding on to what she believes almost as tightly as she holds onto that Koji kid's hand."

"Jealous?"

Ransom snorted softly. "A little envious, maybe. I don't think there's anything or anyone that could come between them ... or between her and her ideals. For someone who cares as much about her reputation as Miss Priss does, to ditch it for Jesus ... ?" With a solemn nod, he said, "That means something."

"I'm glad to hear it, but that doesn't really answer my question," Jayce remarked quietly. "What are you going to do?"

Ransom chuckled nervously. "You holding yourself back, boss? I'd have thought you'd be jumping all over these openings I'm leaving you."

"Believe me, I'm on pins and needles, here. I can listen and advise, but the choice is yours to make."

"No pressure," Ransom muttered with a rueful smile.

Jayce grinned and suggested, "Tell me what you understand."

"I don't have all the right lingo."

"Your own words work just fine," Mr. Pomeroy assured. "I find your perspective refreshing."

"You think?" Ransom replied abashedly. "Well, whatever." He gazed at the ceiling, his thumbs jammed into the upper fold of the apron at his waist. "Sin's a killer, but you can escape. Life's right there for those who are willing to jump for it."

"Jump?"

"Yeah. Like a leap of faith."

"Sure, sure. Go on."

"Right ... so ... this salvation thing is free, but like all stuff in life, there's consequences to my choice. Most of them sound too good to be true."

"Really?"

"My dad always says you get what you pay for," Ransom explained. "Freebies are usually junk."

"True," Jayce conceded, gesturing for him to continue.

"The debts that would have dragged me down to hell are paid, and God takes me in as His own kid. My admission to heaven is covered, and He sticks closer than my closest friend. I'll change ... or be changed. But from what I can tell, people are always changing, so that doesn't worry me much." With a shrug, Ransom said, "And that's about it."

"That does sum it up," Mr. Pomeroy agreed. "So ... ?"

"If what the kids at school have been saying is true, I'd be a fool to even consider Christianity. But if what the Bible says is true, I'd be a fool to believe a little trash-talking." Ransom drew a deep breath, then announced, "God sounds pretty strict but fair, and I like the idea of being part of the same family as you."

"You believe?" Jayce pressed.

"Sure do," Ransom replied seriously.

"Want to make that a formal declaration?"

"Like how?"

"Would it be all right if we prayed together?" Mr. Pomeroy checked.

Ransom cleared his throat. "Yeah, I'd like that."

Looping an arm around the teen's shoulder, Jayce offered a sort of introduction. "Lord God, I know you know all things, but I wanted to bring this boy to you myself. He's been a real help around the shop, and his questions have given me the chance to think through what I believe and why. Thank you for bringing him through my door, but even more, thank you for placing an open door before him." He took a shaky breath and continued in a voice roughened by emotion. "Your Son gave His life as a ransom for many, and *this* Ransom's own name pays tribute to that sacrifice. He's Yours now, Lord. Always and forever."

Ransom jumped right in to the brief lull that followed, saying, "Hey, God ... it's Ransom. All this stuff we've been talking about? I get it. I want it. I'm willing to be yours, and I'm pretty amazed that you'll be mine. So ... yeah. I'm in. All the way. Amen."

Jayce laughed and pulled the boy into a back-slapping hug. "I haven't been this happy since Jude took his leap."

"The kid's already signed on?"

"Jude's a tender-hearted one. He was almost five when he insisted he and Jesus were friends for life."

"Guess I'm getting a late start."

"It's not a race to see who's fastest," Mr. Pomeroy said with a reassuring smile. "We run together, and with each other's help, we can finish well."

"I like the sound of that." Scratching his head, Ransom admitted, "I like how you made my name into something from the Bible. I always figured Mom had a thing for pirates, but I like your explanation better."

"All of my lot have Bible names, too, you know," Mr. Pomeroy revealed.

"No kidding?" Ransom frowned thoughtfully. "Jude I get, but I haven't run across the others yet. Are they in the Old Testament?"

Jayce grimaced. "Come to think of it, the boys are a little sensitive about th–"

Just then, a faint note began to ring from the stainless steel bowls on the shelves as a rumble built in the distance. "Is that thunder?" Ransom asked in a low voice.

The vibrations increased to a chatter, and utensils rattled in their drawers while pots and pans began to shimmy off their shelves, clattering noisily to the floor. "I think it's an earthquake!" Jayce replied, raising his voice to be heard over the din.

"*Here*?"

"There's always a first time."

The tremor tapered off, and Mr. Pomeroy hurried through to the front of the bakery and swung the door wide. Although the sounds were muffled by thickly-falling snow, they could hear dogs barking, car alarms blaring, and the distant wail of sirens. "That was weird," said Ransom.

"It was." With a deep frown, Jayce announced, "I should call home, check on everyone."

"Okay," the teen replied. "Guess I'll put back all the stuff that shook loose."

They were halfway through the swinging door to the kitchen when a heavy knock sounded behind them. Mr. Pomeroy turned back in surprise, then wheeled to unlock for Harken, who stood on the front step. "Afternoon, Jayce," he greeted.

"Harken! Everything okay at your place?"

"Oh, there's nothing to fear," the old shopkeeper replied, waving off any concerns. "I just needed to bring a message."

"From ... ?"

Harken smoothly interjected, "The highway will be closed within half an hour, and you're needed at home. You should leave now."

Mr. Pomeroy hesitated only a moment. "Ransom, we're closing up! Everything else will keep until next year."

The teen drifted over. "Are you sure? I don't mind sticking around to finish up."

"Nope. If it's getting as bad as Harken says, I want to drop you home first," Jayce countered. "I should still be able to...."

"Allow me," Harken interrupted. "I'll make sure the boy gets home safe and sound. You should go."

Mr. Pomeroy glanced at Ransom. "Okay with you?"

"Yeah, sure."

"Fair enough," Jayce acknowledged, then slung an arm around the teen's shoulders. "Though I hate to rush off like this. Harken, this young man has given me an early Christmas present, the best I've received in many a year!"

"Oh?" the shopkeeper inquired.

Ransom smirked. “I’m pretty sure I was the one that got the gift.” Nodding politely to Harken, he explained, “I’m a Christian, sir. Newly minted.”

A broad smile graced Harken’s face, and in a deep voice, he declared, “I say to you, there is joy in the presence of the angels of God over one sinner who repents.” Offering his hand to Ransom, he added, “I’m sure that the heavens are ringing right now, child of God.”

15

THE WHISPERED PRAYER

Prissie opened her eyes to nothingness and gasped in dismay. Darkness pressed around her, and somehow, she knew she wasn't alone. Too afraid to call out, she curled in on herself, ears straining.

"Hello?" came a fragile voice.

"Wh-who's there?"

There was a soft rustle, and the voice murmured, "Calm your heart, Precious. There is nothing for you to fear here."

"Where am I?"

"With me," the voice replied. "I never expected to find *you* in dreams."

"Y-you know who I am?"

"Yes, Prissie. I know you," he replied.

She could hear the smile in his tone, but she wasn't ready to trust. "Do I know you?" she asked nervously.

"No," he sighed. "We have never met, but you are Koji's precious friend. He often speaks of you."

Prissie had no idea *how* she knew, but the epiphany was dazzling. Stretching out her hand, she tentatively whispered, "Ephron?"

Prissie woke with a jolt, but this time she didn't feel as if she were falling. Instead, she was sure she'd been carried away from someplace she wasn't ready to leave. "Wait!" she muttered, reaching desperately toward the ceiling, trying to hold onto the dream. Staring at her upraised hand, which looked pale and gray in the predawn light, she struggled to recall details. This was something important. She knew that much.

Spreading her fingers wide, stretching hard, she found it was just out of reach, disintegrating like mist before the rising sun. Stubbornly, she curled her fingers into a fist, unwilling to let go, not when everything inside her was begging her to heed God's message—trust, listen, remember. "I *can't* remember," she whispered. "I tried, but I just can't remember. If it's so important ... help?"

It wasn't much of a prayer, at least, not by her standards, but when she closed her eyes in frustration, a fragment of a memory seemed to answer her plea. *"Calm your heart, Precious."*

"Ephron!" she gasped. He'd sounded weak, but his words had been kind. He'd known her name and allayed her fears, even though *he* was the one in danger. Prissie's chin trembled, for in a sudden rush, she remembered something else. "Koji asked me...."

Hot shame washed over her, and she hid under her blankets, not wanting anyone—visible or invisible—to see how selfish she'd been. Koji asked for very little, yet she'd withheld something: a prayer for Ephron. The dream had given her a glimpse of his nightmare, and her neglect suddenly felt like a broken promise. Prissie recalled those tunnels, and how terrified she'd been during the brief time she'd been lost in their darkness. Ephron was an angel who longed for the light, yet he'd been hidden from it for months. "I'm sorry," she whimpered. "I'm sorry I forgot!"

Her next prayer came easily, for her brief connection with the captured Observer filled her with urgency. Caring and concern welled up from deep within her soul, and she confessed it all to her Father in heaven. It was embarrassing to admit her failure, even when He knew all her secrets anyhow. Yet she continued until, biting her lip, she muttered a soft, "Amen."

Like a sigh, the worry that had been hanging over her head for weeks whispered away into nothing. Limp with relief, Prissie curled up under her quilts and hoped for the best. If anyone could save Ephron, it was God. She'd done the right thing ... finally.

Dozing lightly, she was startled by a quick tap on her door. Before she could answer, Koji slipped into the room, softly closing the door behind him. He all but flung himself onto the bed. Her surprise quickly turned to alarm, for his cheeks were streaked with tears. Folding her arms around his slender shoulders, she begged, "What's wrong? What's happened?"

The young angel held on tightly, hiding his face as he trembled, but when he finally lifted his gaze to hers, his eyes were shining with joy. "They have been Sent!" he whispered urgently.

"Who has?" she asked, mystified.

"We have!" he replied, smiling through his tears. "Jedrick, Tamaes, and Milo have been *Sent*!"

"Where have they gone?"

"To Ephron," he excitedly answered, wrapping his arms around her for a fierce hug. "They are Sent to bring him back!"

Prissie was too stunned to say a thing. It was so sudden. Almost as if....

A series of thuds and a muffled shout sounded down the hall, soon followed by Tad's voice, then Neil's. Zeke's whoop confused her, since he wasn't usually so noisy this early. Then Jude opened her door, poking his head around the corner. "Aren't you coming?" he asked.

She was still patting Koji's back and hardly knew how to answer. "What's going on?" she finally ventured.

The six-year-old giggled. "Did you forget?"

"What are you talking about?"

With a sunny smile, the littlest Pomeroy announced, "It's Christmas!"

The tiny angel floundered through the darkness, pushing himself to reach the light that sustained him. In the dimness, he blundered into an obstacle and emitted a tiny squeak as two hands closed around him, trapping him. He trembled with exhaustion and fear as he was lifted higher, and a pair of solemn eyes studied his much-dimmed face.

"Well, now," murmured a familiar voice. "This won't do at all."

Lavi blinked through the gaps between long fingers, then managed a soft whimper before sagging to his knees. Abner promptly sat down on the cave floor, humming softly as he ministered to his lost lamb. Light bloomed in the darkness, renewing the yahavim's strength, and the Caretaker smiled in satisfaction as the little one frisked around his head in a dance of thanksgiving.

"It is good to be reminded that even one as small as you can be counted among the Faithful. Go back to Ephron, little lion." With a grim smile, Abner further instructed, "Stay with him until we come; for we, too, have been Sent."

The day was dim, and Prissie was astonished to learn that it was already after eight o'clock when she reached the kitchen. "Has Zeke ever slept this late on Christmas morning?" she wondered aloud.

"Good hibernating weather," Grandma Nell declared, taking a peek into the oven.

Neil breathed deeply as he shrugged into his coat. "Smells good already! Save me some!"

Momma passed Tad a thermos. "Breakfast is in an hour. Try to hurry?"

"Not sure the weather's going to cooperate, but I'll tell Dad and Grandpa," her eldest agreed. "How long have they been out there?"

"Your father woke at his usual time and went out to shovel," Momma replied. "Met your grandfather halfway."

Grandma Nell interjected, "It's blowing bad enough that they strung the guidelines. Use them."

"Yes, ma'am," the boys chorused before heading out into the storm.

Prissie watched from the window. "I can't even see them anymore."

"They are safe," Koji murmured, his dark eyes gazing at the whirl of white beyond the frosted glass.

Momma came up behind them. "They'll only stay out long enough to see to the animals. Koji, I'd like you and Beau to bring in extra firewood ... just in case."

"I will," the young angel quickly agreed. He paused and shyly added, "Merry Christmas."

Mrs. Pomeroy patted his head and warmly returned, "Merry Christmas, Koji."

Even though it was the same every year, Zeke grumbled over having to wait for the real excitement of Christmas to begin. "First things first," Momma soothed. "We'll have all day to play."

"I'll help!" the eight-year-old offered, padding toward his boots in his footie pajamas. "Then the work'll be done faster!"

"Not so fast, young man." His mother collared him and firmly said, "If you want to help, set the table."

Zeke pouted mightily, then drooped. "Yes, ma'am."

"Won't the eggs freeze?" Jude asked worriedly.

"Neil will find them for you today," Momma soothed.

"Does he know all the best places to check?" the six-year-old asked uncertainly.

Grandma Nell laughed. "Gathering eggs was his job when he was your age. He's not likely to forget a hen's tricks."

"Neil likes chickens?" Jude asked, clearly baffled by this new revelation.

Zeke wisely replied, "Sure he does! Especially when Grandma fries 'em."

Eventually, the clock hands crept to the appointed hour,

and the menfolk tromped inside, shedding snow and sharing news. "It's not showing any sign of stopping!" Jayce exclaimed.

"The drift fences are drifted under," Grandpa Pete grumbled. "I'll have to get the tractor out this afternoon."

"It'll keep," Grandma Nell chided.

"Time for stockings?" Zeke pleaded.

Mr. Pomeroy grinned. "Sure, sure ... just as soon as I shake the icicles from my eyebrows."

While the rest of the family bustled around, Prissie edged close to Koji and whispered, "When do you think they'll be back?"

He shook his head. "I do not know."

"They'll be okay ... right?" she pressed.

The young Observer hesitated, then repeated, "I do not know."

Marcus pushed himself, fighting to keep up with his mentor, and Jedrick slowed, ever mindful of his apprentice. "This way," the Flight captain urged, dropping swiftly. Three sets of boots hit the snow, and the young Protector peered at their surroundings. "I know where we are."

"I should think so," Tamaes replied.

"We're still in the orchard?" Marcus asked dubiously. "This *can't* be where Ephron is stashed!"

"No."

"Aww, man! You're leaving me behind?"

Jedrick's smile was sympathetic. "Were you Sent?"

"You know I wasn't," Marcus muttered.

"This is where you will remain," his mentor instructed. "Padgett will see to your safety."

"He's here?" Golden eyes scanned their surroundings, but there was no sign of the Caretaker.

"He is near," Tamaes offered.

Just then, a voice called from behind them, and Marcus whirled to see Milo strolling toward them, barefoot in the snow. The Messenger's wings fluttered in the contrary winds as he said, "We'll be trading places today, Marcus."

"There's no mail to deliver," the younger apprentice pointed out. "National holiday."

"Today was meant to be my last day with Aril," Milo replied seriously. "Thank you for filling in for me."

Marcus's eyes widened in comprehension. "This is ... *that*?"

"It is," Jedrick confirmed.

Padgett joined them then, slipping up without their notice. "Are you prepared?" he inquired. His teammates faced him, and all four nodded. The Caretaker beckoned to Marcus, then looked to Jedrick, simply saying, "Go."

Green, blue, and orange—three sets of wings disappeared into the storm, and Marcus turned to his companion. Padgett's long hair whipped around him, but he paid it no mind. "Come," he invited in a low voice. "I'll introduce you to Aril."

"The Gatekeeper?"

"Few know he is here. Fewer still have met him."

"I knew," Marcus revealed as Padgett opened the way. "Jedrick trusted me with the knowledge, but I was never called upon to...." The young Protector trailed off as he lifted his gaze up, up, and even further upward, to gaze into a pair of fiery orange eyes. When he finally found his voice, he breathed, "*Whoa*!"

The unnatural storm stirred by the fallen Caretaker was devastating, and the whole earth groaned under the weight of his cursed influence. Winds shrilled their complaint, and the ground trembled under his feet.

Fitful gusts tugged at Jedrick's wings, and the very lack of light made it difficult to stay aloft, so he led his teammates straight upward. Together, they fought their way through the wintery maelstrom, bursting through the upper layers of whirling clouds. In the thin air high above the earth, the Protector picked out the weak glimmer of stars that were quickly fading before the pale sunrise. Normally, dawn drove the enemy into deeper shadows, but the current frenzy showed no sign of breaking up. Gruesome warriors screeched and cursed as they raised their weapons against rank upon rank of cherubim, filling the expanse with their clash.

"Have they guessed our purpose?" murmured Milo.

"I doubt it," Jedrick replied in a low voice. "Since the Deep was breached, they have grown bolder."

Tamaes quietly added, "They often test our boundaries. Nights have been long of late."

The Messenger suddenly dropped, neatly avoiding a fiery dart, and Tamaes quickly placed their unarmed companion at his back. With a rueful smile, Milo remarked, "We're attracting attention."

Getting his bearings, Jedrick called, "This way," and tucked his wings close around his body. Without hesitation, the other two plunged after him into the mad rush of the storm, angling to the northeast. Unfortunately, their departure didn't go unnoticed. Dark figures careened after them, the storm rattling through their ragged wings. Turning to fight wasn't an option, so Jedrick sharply ordered, "Faster!"

Milo's answering grin was fierce, and he darted to the fore, blue wings sweeping expertly through the fitful currents. They shot through the scudding snow, arrowing toward Sunderland State Park and the dark gash that rent the earth, the opening to the cave system that would lead them down to the Deep.

Jedrick banked into a tight spiral, but drew up short as soon as he realized that their way was barred. Tamaes hastened to place himself on the other side of Milo as they considered this newest obstacle. "Is that the only entrance?" the Guardian asked.

"Without a Caretaker's intervention ... yes," Jedrick grimly confirmed.

Suddenly, a luminous salvo of arrows cut through the murk, driving back the horde clustered around the entrance to the caves. "Press on!" called the captain whose Flight's bowstrings were already bent for another volley. "The way will also be clear when you return!"

God did not Send without making provision for those Sent. Nodding curtly, Jedrick beckoned for Tamaes and Milo to follow him through the opening they'd created. "Be ready!" he warned, giving his sword a twirl before firming his grip.

"I am prepared," Tamaes answered.

"I, also," Milo affirmed.

As one, they blazed into the darkness.

Prissie found it almost impossible to concentrate on the fun that usually came with opening presents. She kept checking the clock and wondering if her angelic friends were okay. More than once as the day wore on, she found her way to one of the windows to peer out into the storm.

"Whoever prayed up a white Christmas had a heap of faith," her grandfather gruffly announced. "But there's nothing to worry about. We've weathered worse."

With a sigh, Prissie offered Grandpa Pete a meager smile. "I know."

"Then what's troubling you?" pressed the old man. "Did you have your heart set on something that's missing?"

Prissie blinked in surprise at how close he was to the truth, but she quickly assured, "I'm happy with my gifts, Grandpa. I guess I'm just ... thinking about people who couldn't be with us this morning."

"Plenty of folk would have been welcome, but don't lose sight of what's right in front of you by hankering after what could have been." With a significant nod, her grandfather drew her attention to Koji, who was listening with incredible patience as Zeke rambled through a convoluted explanation of the rules to the board game they'd be playing next. "That boy's happiest when you're smiling, and you're being a mite stingy today."

Ducking her head, Prissie replied, "I'll do my best, Grandpa."

He nodded in satisfaction. "That's the way. Give your best, and leave the rest to the good Lord."

Swords flashing, the three angels shot through the cave entrance, bowling over the few Fallen apparently left to keep watch. The demons squealed and scrabbled for cover, spouting profanities at those whose rank in the heavenlies they'd once shared. Chances were good that they'd be bringing reinforcements.

For several long moments, Jedrick, Tamaes, and Milo gazed around the large, central cavern from which Sunderland's innumerable underground passages branched. Without the overhead lighting switched on, the open space was a formless void. While their own wings whispered softly in the stillness, the occasional sour note betrayed the lingering presence of those waiting for their chance.

"Which way?" whispered Milo.

Their captain hesitated, for his directive had only been to get them this far. With an almost apologetic smile, Tamaes stepped into the lead. "Follow me," he announced quietly, pointing deeper down the main artery.

Suddenly, the earth began to shake, and the trio moved so they were back to back, weapons raised. The faint patter of stones echoed in the darkness, temporarily covering any sound of approaching feet, so caution was called for. "More tremors?" Milo muttered. "Abner's not going to be happy."

"True," Jedrick agreed, tensing at the sudden crunch and scuff of footfalls from outside. A double line of cherubim strode into the cave, their wings and raiment bathing the vast chamber with a warm glow that was heaven-sent.

The incoming Flight's captain stepped forward and solemnly declared, "Make the way clear, and it shall remain clear."

"How many are coming?" Jedrick inquired, for warriors continued to sweep through the entrance, bearing swords, spears, and staffs.

With a flick of turquoise wings, the tall archer replied, "As many as it takes to light the way back."

With a grateful heart, Jedrick turned to Tamaes and urged, "Lead on!"

Before they were properly underway, however, Milo skidded to a stop and bowed his head. "It seems that *this* is as far as I will go."

Tamaes turned in surprise and searched his friend's uncharacteristically solemn gaze, then drew a deep breath before nodding. "I will bring Ephron to you. Stand ready."

Six cherubim flanked the lone Messenger, their weapons bristling in every direction as they closed ranks around him. Chuckling softly, Milo promised, "I'll be right here."

Ever downward, ever deeper—Tamaes led the charge, lancing far under the earth on a path that was clear to him, for he was Sent. Every few paces, one of the cherubim following would step to the side, standing guard over some offshoot of the tunnel or simply lending the light of his presence to a dark corner. The way back would be clear, but the way forward grew increasingly difficult.

"Are you certain all those who escaped were returned to their prison?" Tamaes murmured to the captain at his back.

"Quite sure," Jedrick replied as he struggled to use his sword in the close confines of the tunnels. "Save one."

"And these?"

"Future denizens of the Deep," the Protector decreed, the light of battle blazing in his eyes. "Many will be driven before the light and cast into chains before night falls."

"So be it," acknowledged Tamaes, although the battle had yet to be won. Darkness lay before him, sinister and secretive, but he tucked flame-hued wings against his body and pressed forward, defying it to swallow him. Fear had no place in his heart, only concern for the young Observer who'd languished in these depths for too long.

Every step he took brought him closer to the one he felt responsible for losing, yet farther from the one he was responsible to protect. As strange as it felt to leave Prissie in Taweel's watch-care, the voice of God compelled Tamaes. He obeyed, and gladly. Heavy boots beat against the stone floor, crunching on loose pebbles as he ducked and turned, twisting his body through the winding passages that often grew narrow for someone of his stature. All the while, a single refrain sang through his mind—*we are coming, we are coming, we are coming.*

The instant Lavi returned, Ephron knew that the tiny angel had been helped, for he could feel the yahavim's renewed vibrancy. "Did you find your way back to Abner?" With a pang of longing, he admitted, "I miss him ... and the rest."

Enthusiastic fluttering and a generous portion of manna accompanied a hummed melody that spoke to his heart of heaven and hope, and the encouragement was enough to break the prisoner's heart. Without really meaning to, Ephron began to weep. Curling tightly around his faithful little friend, he poured out his sorrow with silently shaking shoulders and shuddering breaths. Lavi patted his cheeks and sang on, a gentle hum that reminded the captive that he wasn't alone ... and never had been.

Soon. The knowledge caught him off guard, and the storm of his emotions stilled. Dabbing at wet cheeks, he cocked his head, listening closely as the promise was repeated.

"Soon," he echoed wonderingly.

Ephron struggled onto his knees and reached up the sides of the pit. The cool stone was rough under his sensitive fingertips, but he'd long since given up on finding a handhold. All the unforgiving wall did was steady him as he pushed shakily to his feet. Straining his ears, he listened intently, and Lavi lapsed into an expectant hush. For quite some time, the heavy silence pressed upon them, but then, in the distance, he caught the growl of voices. Friend or foe? He couldn't tell.

Noises multiplied, and Ephron flinched at the sudden *clang* of metal striking metal. "Did you hear that?" he whispered to Lavi. The yahavim crawled under the collar of the Observer's tattered raiment as the sound of footsteps entered the chamber above the pit. A rock was kicked aside. A blade rasped against its sheath. A pebble tumbled from overhead, plinking off his shoulder before rattling to the floor.

Although it hadn't been thrown with the stinging force Murque liked to use, Ephron's strength left him, and he slid weakly to his knees. Turning his head, he listened to the panting breaths of whoever was looking down at him, and he trembled.

"I found you," came a voice that was deep and dear. "Ephron."

"H-here," he called back, though his voice was little more than a whisper. "I am here."

"I am coming down," Tamaes warned. "Stay against the wall."

Ephron huddled as the air stirred musically through wings whose light he could no longer see. When his teammate's feet connected solidly with the ground, a part of Ephron wanted to hide, but big hands were lifting him. Tamaes quietly announced, "Everyone is waiting. Shall we go?"

"Please," he begged.

Without further ado, the Guardian gathered Ephron close, arranged his wings as best he could in the tight space, and leapt upwards.

The weakened angel gratefully rested his head against Tamaes's shoulder as he strode away from the prison. It was a wonder to Ephron that the way out seemed so easy, for his teammate ran steadily, never hesitating along the convoluted route. Both of Tamaes's hands cradled him close, meaning the big warrior didn't even require his sword.

He was startled by a soft greeting; another soon followed. Ephron whispered, "Who is here?"

"Many," replied Tamaes.

Others called his name, welcoming him back, and the narrow tunnel echoed with an uneven patter as their footfalls multiplied. "So many?" he asked as the unseen warriors fell in step behind.

There was a smile in his teammate's voice as he declared, "The hosts of heaven shine like stars underground. I wish you could see."

Touching the makeshift bandages covering his eyes, Ephron murmured, "Tell me?"

Tamaes kept his voice low as he shared the names, colors, and Flight placements of the cherubim who washed their route in light, protecting them from behind, leading them home.

Time passed slowly, the way grew steep in places, and eventually, the tunnel widened. "Are we close?" Ephron asked.

"We are," Tamaes acknowledged, slowing to a stop in order to listen. The roar of battle reached back to them, warning them that they would have to fight for their freedom. Ephron curled more tightly against his rescuer, whose grasp tightened reassuringly.

"Let us pass," urged the Protector just behind Tamaes's shoulder.

Tucking Ephron into the folds of his wings, the Guardian pressed himself against the wall, allowing the flood of cherubim to precede them into the main cavern. Tamaes followed more slowly and spoke in soothing tones. "Milo is waiting for us," he shared.

"Oh," Ephron breathed wistfully. "I am glad."

"And Jedrick," the Guardian added, adjusting his grip so he could draw his sword. "Naturally."

"Yes, of course."

Tamaes stopped walking, and Ephron shrank against him, unnerved by the noise. The Guardian hummed soothingly, then confidently said, "Your safe return is assured. Fear not."

"I will trust."

"Good," the big warrior replied before plunging into the melee.

Milo gratefully clasped Jedrick's arm when the Protector returned to his side. Without preamble, the Flight captain said, "I am moving you to the entrance."

"Now?" The Messenger allowed himself to be herded along the wall toward the mouth of the cave, but he peered back over his shoulder. "Aren't they coming?"

"They are," Jedrick confirmed. "Tamaes will bring Ephron to you."

"Is he all right?"

"Ephron is terribly faded," the Protector solemnly replied. "You will need to carry him."

"Not you?" Milo countered in honest surprise.

"You are the swiftest in our Flight. I will prevent any from following you."

"*We*," interjected one of the half dozen cherubim who'd been protecting the Messenger.

"We," Jedrick amended, nodded his acknowledgment to the angels who moved with them. To Milo, he said, "You will have a head start. Use it."

The Messenger's wings shifted restlessly, then rose defensively as a volley of stones was flung their way. "I can't think of another delivery I'd rather make today," he assured. "I'll be ready."

After a brief skirmish, they gained the entrance, putting them back within reach of the blizzard. The short winter day was ending, so the sting of driven snow hurled into them out of the darkness. Jedrick crossed blades with a screeching demon whose tattered wings dragged uselessly upon the ground, while another of the cherubim squared off with a squat demon with a glittering dagger. "Make ready!" the Captain shouted.

Milo wheeled in time to see Tamaes launch out of the inner recesses of the cavern, his orange wings tucked close around his precious cargo. Immediately, the Messenger let slide the restraints that became second nature to Grafts. Holding nothing back, his face shone like lightning, filling every nook and cranny of the passage with a radiance borne of heaven. Those Fallen who were nearest cried out and stumbled backward, but Tamaes's urgent gaze zeroed in on Milo. Seizing the opportunity his teammate's short burst created, the Protector flung his wings wide and charged right over the top of the mingled ranks. A few weapons stabbed blindly upward, but other angels intervened, knocking aside their blows.

Stumbling to his knees before the Messenger, Tamaes sucked in his breath, then gently shook his passenger. "Ephron, we are here. You need to go with Milo now."

"Milo?"

"Right here," answered the Messenger, catching hold of the Observer's hand. "Upsy-daisy!" The transfer was clumsy, but Ephron soon had his arms wrapped tightly around Milo's neck. Bouncing on the balls of his feet, he stretched wide his blue wings. "It's been a while since I had a passenger," he confessed. "Bear with me?"

Jedrick's voice cut him off. "Fly to Abner!"

Taking a deep breath, Milo prepared to hurl himself into the storm, but to his amazement, the winds stilled and the sky opened up, giving him a clear view of the sky overhead.

"What happened?" Ephron asked, turning his head this way and that.

"*Abner* happened," Milo replied with a grin. "Thanks be to God for His mercy ..." The Messenger trailed off with a stunned, "Have mercy!"

The Observer's hold tightened so that he was practically throttling his friend. "What do you see?" he asked tensely.

"Abner," Milo replied distractedly.

"Go!" growled Jedrick, giving the startled Messenger's shoulder a shove.

Milo obediently took flight, and one after another, the six cherubim Sent to watch over him followed suit. Jedrick also soared skyward, then turned to check for pursuers, wings widespread as he surveyed the scene just below. He gestured broadly for Prissie's Guardian to follow, but his expression quickly shifted into one of dismay. "Tamaes!" Jedrick urgently called. "Behind you! *Fly*!"

Creeping shadows coalesced, catching at the auburn-haired angel's ankles and winding through his wings. Before the Guardian could jerk free, spines encircled him from behind, the decrepit wingtips locking around him in a creaking cage. "Hello, Tamaes," a smooth voice greeted.

"Adin," Tamaes stiffly acknowledged.

"Ever the fool," his former comrade said smugly. "How does it feel to be betrayed by the One you serve?"

Tamaes's features hardened into grim lines. "Is that what you think?"

"I know it!"

"Then *you* are the fool," the Guardian calmly retorted, despite the crushing grip that prevented him from raising his sword.

"The God of heaven Sent you into darkness," Adin mocked, his eyes flashing briefly to the seven cherubim hovering just overhead. With a sneer, he dragged Tamaes backward, promising, "In darkness you shall remain."

16

THE ROUGH NIGHT

Usually, Prissie loved a long day of puzzles and board games, but she was having the worst time fitting in with her family's diversions. She could feel the long looks Koji was sending her way, but so far, she'd been dodging them. Momma noticed the difference. "Are you feeling okay, sweetie?"

"I'm fine." It wasn't exactly a lie, but it felt like one. Managing a brighter expression, she said, "I think I'll follow Tad's example and take a little nap."

Her mother relaxed. "I might do the same. Go on, then."

Prissie slipped from the kitchen, escaping up the back stairs, but she didn't go all the way to her room. Instead, she chose a spot halfway up and sat on a step, hugging herself in the dim passage. The storm seemed to have smothered all the sunlight, but it wasn't as dark as her dream had been. Shivering at the memory, she bowed her head and wished for a way to know what was happening to her friends.

A soft sound made her glance up, and she saw Koji peeking his head around the corner below, his dark eyes uncertain as he gazed up at her. With a sigh, she waved him over, and he tiptoed lightly up to join her on the stairs. "Why are you grieving?" he asked.

"The place where Ephron is," she ventured. "It's dark there."

He cocked his head quizzically, but replied, "Yes."

"I saw," she explained, then shook her head. "I mean ... I couldn't see."

Koji's eyes widened somewhat, but then his gaze softened. "When did you meet?"

"This morning. Just before...."

Nudging closer, he asked, "Were you afraid?"

"A little." Leaning her arm against his, she mumbled, "Or ... a lot. I still am."

"Why?" the young angel inquired. "We have been Sent."

Knotting her fingers together, she asked, "Do you know what's happening?"

"No."

"Don't you usually keep up with each other ... somehow?" she pressed. "I thought you could talk to each other in your heads ... or something?"

"Neither Harken nor Milo have conferred with me this day," Koji reported gravely. "Would you like me to see if they have good tidings?"

"Would you?" she pleaded. "Something's *strange* about today. I don't like this storm!"

"Indeed," he agreed. "I will see if anyone is listening."

"Thank you," Prissie whispered.

Koji hesitated, then admitted, "It is easier for me in dreams. Would you be my Guardian for a time?"

There was a sparkle in his eyes, and Prissie suspected he was making a joke. "If I have to," she replied, fond in her exasperation. To her surprise, he nestled closer, resting his head against her shoulder and letting his eyes drift shut. Suddenly self-conscious, she whispered, "Here?"

He hummed softly and reached for her hand. "Yes, please."

Prissie quickly wrapped her arm around him, holding him up as he slipped into dreams. It was almost like a hug, and then it became a hug because she needed something to hold onto. Her arm tightened around Koji's shoulders, and she laid her cheek atop his head and hoped his news would be good. Her conscience twinged, and with chagrin, she closed her eyes and prayed it would be good as well.

Slowly, the worst of her fears ebbed away, for Prissie found that clinging to faith was easier when you embraced a citizen of heaven. Somehow, everything would turn out okay. It just *had* to.

Right before dinner, Neil thudded down the back stairs, nearly bowling over Prissie and Koji. The sixteen-year-old yelped, "Whoa, you two! What's with the road block?"

Prissie blinked blearily at her brother. Koji hadn't stirred in so long that she'd almost dozed off herself. Ignoring the question, she took in Neil's plaid pajama pants and oversized sweatshirt and guessed he'd been relaxing in his room. He was far from relaxed, though. Eyes wide and hands shaking, he was almost beside himself. "Is something wrong?" she asked.

"Uhh ... kinda, but keep it down," he replied with a grimace. "I need to talk to Dad."

With that, he angled past them and hurried on through the kitchen door. Koji roused, and Prissie let her arms fall to her sides as he straightened, gazing intently after Neil. "Things are happening," the young Observer said, his expression pensive.

"What kinds of things?"

Shaking his head, Koji announced, "Harken said to stay with you."

"Weren't you doing that anyhow?"

"Indeed."

"Fine," she sighed. "Come on, let's see what Neil's all worked up about."

Prissie glanced at the clock on her way through the kitchen, where Grandma Nell was already starting to pull together leftovers for a late supper. Neil was dragging their father into the tiny adjoining office space, and without a second thought, she followed.

Her older brother glared at her, but he didn't tell her to get lost. Instead, he held a warning finger to his lips, and in some distant part of her mind, Prissie appreciated the show of trust on Neil's part. She would be in on this secret.

Jayce's attention was fixed on Neil. "Son?"

"R-right," he replied, scrubbing at his face before rambling into an explanation. "So ... I was upstairs, and I had the scanner on. It's kind of a mess out there today. All kinds of trees down, power outages, damage to buildings, broken windows at Trinity, spin-outs ... and stuff."

"Sure, sure." Dad eyed his son with a trace of confusion. Prissie had never seen Neil so pale and subdued, and a knot formed in her stomach. The teen rubbed the back of his neck and seemed uncertain how to go on, so their dad coaxed, "What is it, Son?"

"There's a fire." His voice cracked as he continued, "They gave the address ... on Main Street. Dad, it's the bakery."

After a hushed conference with his wife and parents, Jayce closed himself into the small office in order to make some calls, but he reappeared within moments. "The line's dead, and I can't get a signal. It must be the storm."

"What should we do?" Naomi asked quietly.

A gust of wind rattled the windows in their frames, and Mr. Pomeroy stared at the whirl of white beyond. "I know there's nothing I can do, but I want to head into town. See for myself."

"I'll go with you," Neil immediately offered.

Grandpa Pete folded his arms over his chest, his expression grim. "It's a fool's errand, but if you insist on going, take the tractor."

"To town?" Momma gasped.

The old man replied, "Slow and steady ... and a long sight safer than slip-sliding around out there in one of the cars."

Mrs. Pomeroy glanced between her husband and her father-in-law, then nodded. "Bundle up."

"I'll fill a couple of thermoses," Grandma Nell interjected. "And you should eat something first."

"Don't think I can manage that," Jayce wryly admitted.

"I'll change," Neil announced, jogging past Prissie and Koji toward the stairs.

Momma pursed her lips. "Prissie, go wake Tad and tell him to come to the kitchen. I'll grab Beau. I think we'll wait to tell the little boys, though. Let them have their Christmas."

"Yes, ma'am," Prissie murmured, moving rather numbly into the family room. What would they do if Dad lost the bakery? Shaking her head, she hoped there was some mistake, but then Koji's fingers grazed her hand. One look at his face, and she knew it was true. Things were happening ... and they were all *bad*.

In the family room, Tad sprawled on one of the couches, sound asleep while Zeke and Jude played together on the floor in front of the wood stove. Prissie smiled a little when she noticed that her big-big brother was putting her gift to use. Tad was forever bunching up his jacket to prop his head during his impromptu naps. After lengthy consideration, she'd bought him a small travel-sized pillow and sewn a pillowcase out of flannel. Kneeling next to him, she gave his shoulder a small shake.

Tad woke, and his gray eyes went from sleepy to solemn in a twinkling. "Priss?"

"Dad needs to talk to you," she replied, trying to act normally. "In the kitchen."

He pushed himself up onto his elbows, still scrutinizing her face. "Is it bad?" he murmured. Her lip trembled, and he nodded once, rolling to his feet and striding purposefully to the kitchen.

Prissie dropped limply onto the couch, and Koji joined her. "What's going on?" she whispered.

The young angel pondered the matter, then admitted, "More than I can know, let alone understand."

By unspoken agreement, Grandpa and Tad took charge of Zeke and Jude, coaxing the boys back to the family room in order to pop corn and roast apples over the embers in the wood stove. The bedtime snack would signal the end of a long day of fun for them, but the atmosphere was noticeably subdued. At Momma's request, Beau moved Neil's scanner to the kitchen, and she and Grandma Nell took over one end of the long table with a jigsaw puzzle and a fresh pot of coffee.

While Beau fiddled with the scanner settings, Prissie drifted to the table, needing something to take her mind off the waiting. Her angelic friends had been gone since sunrise, and Dad and Neil had been gone for nearly two hours. Momma would bow her head or murmur something under her breath, but praying didn't seem to be hurrying things along. "How much longer?" Prissie sighed.

"If they're smart, they'll stay in town until morning," Grandma Nell offered. "Mr. Mercer would put them up."

Prissie straightened and looked at Koji, who stood at the kitchen window, transfixed by sights she couldn't see. She saw the young Observer grab hold of the window sill with a white-knuckled grip. It was the only warning she had, for in the next instant, lightning flashed dazzlingly, immediately followed by the crash and boom of thunder directly overhead. The whole house rattled, and the power went out, leaving the Pomeroys in stunned silence.

Grandma Nell patted her heart and briskly said, "I'll get more candles."

Screeching tones and static caused Prissie to jump and

look at Beau accusingly. Her brother shrugged at the scanner. "It has batteries."

Jude trotted into the kitchen, making straight for his mother's arms. "Do you think Maddie's okay?" he asked worriedly.

Grandpa, who'd followed close on the boy's heels, answered, "The coop has a good foundation, so even if she's fussed, she's safe. Kinda like us."

As Tad and Zeke sidled into the room, Prissie scooted over to join Koji at the window. Another blaze of lightning forced her to squint, but once it gave way to a deep roll of thunder, her eyes widened in disbelief. "How is that possible?" she whispered.

"Nothing is impossible," answered Koji.

"Well, I never!" muttered Grandpa Pete, who promptly headed for the back door to get a better look.

The Pomeroys crowded onto the back porch to stare up at the whirl of clouds surrounding their farm. They were in the eye of the storm, and the sky above had opened up, revealing stars overhead. Prissie had no idea what her family was seeing, but on every side, colors flashed and darted, driving back the shadows. Angels were doing battle, keeping the enemy at bay. "We're safe!" she gasped.

Another rumble began to build in the distance, and Tad grimly said, "I don't think that's thunder."

"Is there gonna be a tornado?" demanded Zeke, staring around with an awed expression.

Vibrations shook the porch, and Grandma Nell exclaimed, "An earthquake?"

Just then, a bolt zoomed across the sky, colliding with the barn, and its lightning rods danced with electricity.

"Basement! Now!" Momma called, her voice ringing with authority.

They hadn't needed to take shelter since early summer, when tornado warnings had sent them down below. The storm cellar was always stocked for emergencies, though the space wasn't due for an airing out until spring. Tad led the way, calmly grabbing hold of Zeke's arm before the youngster could run off. "You heard Momma," he scolded.

"But my stuff!" the eight-year-old protested.

"It'll keep," Tad said with a sympathetic smile. "Come on, Jude. You bring Momma."

"'Kay!" agreed the youngest Pomeroy, who was holding tight to Naomi's hand.

Grandpa Pete helped Grandma Nell snuff the scattered candles, then escorted her downstairs as well, but Prissie lingered by the door with Koji. Blinding flashes danced along the edges of the whirlwind, as if they were being held back from striking the farm buildings. Each strobe cast their orchard into stark relief, black trees against white snow; however, they brought something else to Prissie's attention.

Something was moving in the orchard, and it was *big.* A spate of sleet cut through the air, stinging her cheeks, but she lingered, staring hard as she waited for the next flash. When it came, she almost couldn't make sense of what she was seeing.

"Coming, Priss?" called Beau.

"J-just a minute," she answered, giving her brother a pleading look.

"You shouldn't be in the open," he warned, hesitating at the top of the basement stairs.

Lightning blazed again, and Prissie's gaze swung back to

the orchard. The winds dropped, and in the strange stillness, she could hear noises—creaking, groaning, cracking. "Oh, no!" she moaned. "The trees!"

"It cannot be helped," Koji remarked, his gaze fixed on a struggle of epic proportions.

Not one colossus, but two grappled in the midst of the orchard. The giants stood taller than the barn and its silos, and as they pushed and pulled against each other, apple trees snapped like twigs beneath their feet. Even though the scale boggled her mind, Prissie recognized the sweep of silver hair that swayed behind the brighter of the two figures. "That's Abner," she gasped.

"Indeed."

While her Caretaker friend's raiment shone as brightly as ever, his opponent seemed to be draped in rags; they hung from the gaunt frame of a demon with wild eyes that held nothing but hate. Abner's hand was firmly planted over the enemy's mouth, preventing him from uttering a sound. "Is he the one responsible for the storm?" she asked. "Does that mean Abner is stopping him?"

Koji solemnly said, "He will not let the enemy speak, for his words are like poison."

From behind them, Beau asked, "What are you guys looking at?"

"What can you see?" she asked nervously.

"Not much," he admitted, trying to follow her gaze.

The wrestling match continued over precious acreage, and she murmured, "Is there anything we can do?"

"You can pray," Koji gently replied.

Prissie glanced nervously at Beau, who frowned deeply at something in the distance. Shaking her head, she whispered, "For *what*?"

From amid the swirl of colors, a single streak of blue cut into the open sky, swift as a comet … or a falling star to wish upon. Gripping her hand fiercely, Koji pointed urgently, exclaiming, "For them!"

"Is that … ?" A rolling cloud of malice pursued that single beam of light, and Prissie's hand clapped over her mouth lest she blurt out anything in front of Beau.

Her brother's eyes narrowed, and he muttered, "Is that a meteor or something?"

"Kids!" their mother called urgently, her voice carrying up the basement stairs. "Come down here!"

"Hang on, Momma!" Prissie called back, her eyes fixed on Milo's wavering flight pattern.

Koji's took a half-step forward, eyes wide with concern. "He is fast, but his burden is great."

"Where are the others?" she wailed, no longer caring if Beau heard. "Can't they help?"

"They are," he assured. "They part before him and close ranks behind him."

The streak grew close enough that Prissie could make out Milo's wings. They were tucked close to his body, giving him a streamlined appearance as he dove toward safety. Nervously, Prissie asked, "Shouldn't he be slowing down about now?"

"Prissie," Beau interrupted, his wide eyes fixed on the oncoming angel. "That thing's gonna hit!"

"Y-you can see him?" she gasped.

"*Him*?" he echoed, shooting her a look of utter confusion.

A crack like thunder split the night, and the earth trembled underfoot as something crashed into the house, rattling it to its foundations. Momma's voice came again. "Kids! Are you all right?"

"Yeah!" Beau answered, his face pale in the beam of the flashlight he clicked on. "Something hit the house, but don't worry! I'll check it!"

"No!" Momma countered, but it was too late. The teen had already dashed up the back stairs, Koji right behind him. Prissie had no choice but to follow.

"Come back!" her mother called.

For the first time in longer than she could remember, Prissie flat-out disobeyed her mother. If Koji needed to stay with her, then that meant she needed to stay with Koji. Holding her skirts high, she followed as quickly as she could in the darkness, mentally counting the stairs as she fumbled upwards.

From the top step, she could already tell something was very wrong. The upstairs hallway was quiet enough for her to hear the strange whistling of the wind. Cold as ice, it slithered past her ankles, seeping into the house from the direction of her bedroom.

The door with its quirky angled top hung open, and an eerie blue light filtered through into the hallway. Prissie tiptoed closer, afraid to look, yet needing to know. Firming her resolve, she stepped through the door.

At first, all she could do was gape at the wreckage. It was far worse than she could have imagined, for she could see the stars through what was left of her ceiling. Tree branches poked and twisted every which way, and snowflakes drifted through on faint gusts of wind. Her braided rug was littered with broken glass, and in the middle of the mess, Beau knelt beside the sagging figure propped against one wall.

The light she'd seen wasn't coming from the moon. Luminous blue wings were draped at odd angles, and they lent a soft glow to the room. Beau's fists were clenched at his sides, and he looked over his shoulder at her. "I know this is gonna sound crazy, Priss, but this guy looks a whole lot like Milo."

She took a shuffling step forward, bits of colored glass crunching under her slippers. "It's not crazy," she managed, her voice wavering. "He's obviously Milo."

The Messenger's eyes fluttered open, and he wheezed, "Hey there, Boaz. Please … don't be afraid."

Beau nodded dumbly, then shook his head.

"It looks like someone threw a tree at the house," Prissie muttered.

Koji, who was now clad in raiment, stepped to her side and calmly corrected, "He was aiming for Milo."

Prissie dragged her attention to their mailman, and her dismay reached new heights. "You're bleeding!" she exclaimed, hurrying to his side.

"Sorry for the mess," Milo replied with a wan smile. His ash blond curls were in wild disarray, and he pressed one hand to his side. He seemed to be dimming, and his eyelids drooped.

"Padgett is coming," Koji quietly announced.

"S'good," the Messenger mumbled before slipping into unconsciousness.

"Wings?" Beau interjected, shaking his head in disbelief. "Are you telling me these are wings? Like … like an angel?"

"Just like," Prissie crisply replied, growing more frightened by the moment. Suddenly, she noticed the waif tucked against Milo's side, half-hidden by the drape of one wing. A pallid face streaked with dirt and tears lifted slightly, turning toward their voices. Prissie immediately spotted a pointed ear poking through ragged hair, but was more disturbed by the strips of cloth that wound across his eyes. Thin hands fisted tightly into Milo's tunic as he offered a weak, "F-fear not?"

In the awkward silence, Koji calmly stepped forward and knelt before the newcomer, slipping his arms around trembling shoulders and warmly declaring, "Welcome back, Ephron."

The story concludes in Book 4: The Garden Gate....

DISCUSSION QUESTIONS FOR BOOK 3

During the Christmas Open House at the bakery, Padgett remarks, "Letting emotions dictate your decisions can be as unwise as letting appearances influence your opinions." Do your head and your heart ever disagree? How important are first impressions? Why are second impressions worthwhile?

Who's the trickiest person on your gift list? Why are they hard to shop for? What about you ... do you like practical or impractical gifts?

When Prissie dreams that she's in the hayloft, she sees scores of injured angels. Those Protectors and Guardians have always been nearby, but until now, she didn't give a thought to the dangers they face for her sake. "The more she met, the more she cared." Why does knowing come before caring? Stop and think. Are there strangers you're taking for granted?

April Mayfair is caught in the middle of a frenemy feud. She tries to stay neutral, but Prissie ends up feeling betrayed. Have you ever been stuck in April's shoes? Why is it such a tricky place to be?

During his message, Pastor Denny Kern of the DeeVee says, "I can hear you now, saying, 'It's no big deal, Denny. Don't sweat the small stuff!'" Can little things be important? Can you name a small thing that hurt you deeply? Is there a little thing that always brightens your day?

Prissie points out, "Lots of people wish they could fly like a bird. Or that they had super powers or magical abilities." What about you?

Koji is an Observer, but watching isn't enough for him. Prissie admires the way he throws himself into new experiences. How brave are you about trying new things? We all have stuff we refuse to attempt. Where do you draw the line?

Would you rather know the truth, even if it was hard to accept ... or put your faith in an appealing lie?

- Prissie admits that what she wants most is to matter to Milo and Koji as much as they mattered to her. Who matters to you? Who do you want to matter to? Who wants to matter to you?

- "One never knows what God can use. Even if I do not understand the purpose of a thing, that does not mean it has none." Can you think of something you thought was useless but came in handy later?

- Have you ever taken part in a white elephant gift exchange? What would you bring if you were invited to one?

- At Christmas, Grandpa Pete says, "Don't lose sight of what's right in front of you by hankering after what could have been." What's right in front of you?

THRESHOLD SERIES GLOSSARY

Praise the Lord, you his angels,
you mighty ones who do his bidding,
who obey his word.
– Psalm 103:20 NIV

ORDER OF ANGELS

Orders of Angels. They're variously called the hosts of heaven (Neh. 9:6), powers and principalities (Rom. 8:38), thrones and dominions (Col. 1:16), angels and authorities (1 Pet. 3:22), and ministering spirits (Heb. 1:14). Throughout the *Threshold Series* and its various companion stories, I've divided these servants of God into distinct orders. While their characteristics are inspired by the Scriptures, bear in mind that these varieties are the author's invention. Each of their proper names is spun from a Hebrew word related to the order's unique role ... and parallels those of the two kinds of angels specified in the Bible — cherubim (Ex. 25:22) and seraphim (Is. 6:2).

Protectors. In the Bible, cherubim are protectors of God's name and image. They're usually described as beings who devote themselves to blessing, praising, and adoring Him. In my stories, Protectors fight the Fallen. Taller than humanly possible, these muscular warriors are well-equipped for battle.

Guardians. The hadarim watch over the lives of individuals. The Guardians' name is taken from *haderes,* which means "hedge of protection." In the *Threshold Series,* members of this order are famously bashful and show incredible fierceness when defending their charges.

Messengers. Malakim comes from *malak,* which means "messenger." They're responsible for communication within the ranks of heaven, and they're known for being outgoing and talkative. Language poses no barrier for Messengers. Members of this order are skilled at drawing others into dreams and visions.

Worshipers. The zamarim derive their name from *zamar,* "sing with instruments." Although all angels express themselves through song, Worshipers truly live to praise God with everything they have. One thing that sets apart this order of musically inclined angels is their wings, which are designed more for beauty than for flight.

Observers. The archivists of heaven are adahim. They get their name from *adah,* "to witness, to testify." Observers watch the intricate plans and purposes of God unfold throughout history. Writers, thinkers, artists, poets — the adahim ponder all they've seen and heard and record their thoughts in books.

Caretakers. Earth-movers and storm-bringers, the samayim were granted cataclysmic power in order to care for the created universe. There's very little a Caretaker cannot do, but at the same time, they're limited in what they're allowed to do. In the *Threshold Series,* the samayim show an affinity for nature, minister to the injured, change the physical appearances of people, and tend flocks of yahavim. Their name means "heavens."

Manna-makers. Despite their diminutive size and playful nature, all the hosts of heaven depend heavily upon the yahavim. This lowest order of angels is responsible for producing manna, the food of angels. Their name comes from *yahav,* which means "provide." They're drawn to those in need.

ANGELIC TERMS

Angelic Jargon. Several terms come up over the course of the *Threshold Series,* and while the angels take them for granted, maybe you'd like a little more explanation.

The First. In this storyline, not all angels were created at the same time. Some have been around for millennia, but others are newly formed. When an angel is described as one of the First, it means that he was alive before Time began. First Ones remember the rift that divided the Fallen from the Faithful, and they witnessed creation of the heavens and earth as described in Genesis 1.

Faithful. An angel who lives to serve God.

Fallen. An angel who has set himself against God. Fallen angels are demons.

Mentor. When an older, wiser angel is given a newbie to train, he becomes their mentor. A small, silvery cuff on the shell of the left ear indicates their rank. Mentors may train several apprentices over their lifetime, but only one at a time.

Apprentice. When angels are Sent out of heaven to serve, they always go in pairs. Sometimes, these two-angel teams involve partners on equal footing, but more often, a newer angel is apprenticed to a mentor. Some apprentices end up partnering with several different mentors before their training is considered complete.

Legion. For the purposes of this storyline, one Legion is a company of 12,000 angels.

Flight. The Faithful are organized into twelve-angel teams that are headed up by a captain. That means a Legion is comprised of 1,000 Flights.

Hedge. A group of Guardians serving together in one area is called a Hedge. The hadarim form a perimeter around individual homes, but also in crowded places — schools, apartment buildings, businesses, shopping centers, concerts, sporting events, etc. Because guardian angels come and go whenever their charges do, Hedges are in a constant state of flux.

Graft. When an angel takes on human guise and becomes a part of society, he's said to be grafted in.

Raiment. The Faithful wear raiment, clothing said to have a light and life of its own. The woven fabric is beige, faintly luminous, and resistant to spot and wrinkle. Design varies slightly depending on the needs of the wearer, and the patterns stitched on the collar and cuffs indicate flight, rank, and order.

THRESHOLD SERIES

THE GARDEN GATE

BOOK FOUR

1

THE BROKEN PIECES

Two colossal angels wrestled in the darkness, trampling snow and upturning frozen earth as neat rows of apple trees crunched beneath their feet. Lightning blazed, momentarily illuminating the hatred glittering in the narrowed eyes of a Fallen whose dingy clothes flapped against a gaunt frame. Sagging folds of skin bunched as his jaw worked, but a clean, bright hand kept the demon from unleashing pent up curses. Abner's lips tightened into a grim smile. "Your mouth is sealed, as is your fate."

With a growl, the Fallen drove his shoulder into his captor's ribs, twisting away. Great feet snapped more branches, and the chains that dragged from shackled ankles nearly collided with the Pomeroys' machine shed. "You've done enough damage," Abner said, steering his opponent away from snow-covered barns.

They vied for control of the freakish blizzard that had buried most of West Edinton under snow and ice. Storm clouds threatened to close in, but their dark spiral left the angels—and much of the Pomeroys' farm—bare to the brittle light of stars. Thunder rolled, and varicolored streaks blazed across that wide patch of night sky in tight formations, then scattered into dizzying patterns as they drove back the shadows. Other Flights veered lower, skimming along the tops of trees, driving stragglers before the points of spear and sword.

Abner's grip shifted, and he pressed down on his opponent. The diminishing demon renewed his struggle as the Caretaker reshaped him, robbing him of the power that came with sheer mass. They shrank to the size of mere mortals, and Abner invited, "Take one last look at the expanse of heaven before I return you to darkness."

In that instant, the fearsome storm lost its strength, and the clouds dispersed, washing their corner of the world with the silvery light of the moon. Peace spelled defeat, but not an end to the Fallen's defiance. Wrenching free, he lunged for Abner's throat; however, a passage opened beneath the demon's feet. Chains rattled against the pit's edge as the Deep swallowed him, and his howl of impotent fury cut short when the earth resealed itself.

The triumphant Caretaker clasped his hands behind his back and turned to look at the darkened farmhouse. Tree roots protruded from the roof above one of the gables, and blue light bled through jagged gaps, outlining the wreckage of Prissie Pomeroy's bedroom. Destruction. Pain. Suffering. Abner was willing to go, but this time, he was not Sent.

Snow sifted down between jutting boards and dangling shingles as Prissie crept deeper into the remains of her sanctuary. Trailing tufts of pink insulation hung from the bare branches of an uprooted apple tree, which left her room smelling like soil.

Beau turned to her, hand upraised; bright liquid slicked his fingertips. "This is ... ?"

Prissie shivered. "He's bleeding."

Her younger brother frowned down at Milo. "Is first aid the same for angels?"

How could he be taking this so calmly? Prissie caught sight of a cracked sphere of pink glass surrounded by more delicate shards. Her ornament collection. Spoiled. Gone.

"Sis?" When she looked, Beau tensely begged, "Help me stop the bleeding."

Prissie joined her brother, kneeling carefully on the unconscious angel's other side. "Milo?" she called in a low voice. The Messenger's torn raiment glowed more brightly in the damp places where it clung to wounds, and a thin trickle dribbled down the side of his face. "Please, Milo!"

Beau plunged right in, putting pressure against the gash in their mailman's side. "Like this?"

"I think so. I hope so," Prissie replied uncertainly, pressing her hand over Milo's shoulder.

"Do not fear," Koji said. "Padgett is coming."

"Oh, thank God," she whispered, meaning it with all her heart. They needed help. No, Milo needed help. "Yes, please. Send Padgett."

"You know, Milo was my favorite Sunday school teacher. He told the best stories, made us think, made them real. I could tell he really cared about the Bible." Beau stared at their long-time friend, who looked pretty strange with his long curls and outspread wings. "He believed in God like nobody else I've ever met, and I wanted to be like that. To believe like that."

"He's still Milo," Prissie muttered.

Her brother smiled shakily. "Yeah. He's still everything he seemed to be, but the reasons are different. Better. This is perfect."

Such a different reaction than her own. But then, her younger brothers knew him in a different way than she did. "Was he really that good a teacher?"

"The best. Absolute best," Beau replied fervently. "I'd go back to being Zeke's age if I could. Just to keep him."

Suddenly, a door opened out of nowhere, and another angel stepped into the room, his gaze taking in the whole scene. "Padgett!" Prissie struggled to her feet. Her throat threatened to close, but she choked out, "Milo's hurt!"

Some of the fierceness left the Caretaker's face as he quickly crossed to her side, his long, black hair sweeping across the debris scattering the floor. "Don't worry, miss. That's why I was Sent."

"Can you help him?"

Padgett touched her face. "Fear not. None of the Faithful are beyond help. Trust God to provide."

She felt a little steadier, a little calmer, and she suspected him of ministering to her on a divine level. "Not me! Him!"

"Them," Koji quietly corrected, for his arms still sheltered Ephron.

"Of course," Padgett replied, crossing to the Messenger, whose wings still provided the brightest light in the surrounding darkness.

Beau gawked up at the newcomer. "Can you really help Milo?"

"Yes."

"That's good. Thanks."

Padgett's hands moved without haste—smoothing, straightening, strengthening. "Do not thank me. Thank God."

"Have been," Beau replied.

The Caretaker paused in his work. "Milo is important to you."

"Yeah. He's my friend."

"He's also mine."

Beau checked, "Are you really an angel?"

"Yes."

"Wow."

Padgett's almost-there smile made an appearance, and he reached across to touch the top of Beau's head. "Don't be afraid. Everything is in God's hands."

Beau offered a small nod and asked, "Can I help?"

"Thank you." The Caretaker reached into one of his wide sleeves and produced a roll of softly-glowing gauze, which he passed to the teen. Catching Prissie's eye, Padgett nodded significantly toward Koji.

There was no refusing the implied request, but she felt the need to ask, "What will Momma say when she comes looking for us?"

"We have all the time we need."

Prissie's eyebrows slowly lifted. "Did you do something?"

Padgett patiently answered, "I've prolonged this moment so we can finish without causing further distress to your family."

With one less worry weighing on her mind, she glanced at Koji, who had his hands full with a shivering bundle of skin and bones draped in torn raiment. She shuffled her slippers across the braided rug, cringing with every crunch of glass underfoot, to pull a soft blanket off the bed. Shaking it out, she made her way to Koji. Angels might not feel cold, but her friend couldn't offer Ephron the shelter of wings. When she draped her substitute around the pale angel's shoulders, he started.

Koji spoke in low tones. "Prissie is with us. You remember her. She is my friend. You are safe with us. We are with you." His soft assurances had a lilting quality that soon became a song that promised peace and comfort.

Even though Ephron was clearly taller than the younger Observer, he'd curled into a tight, defensive ball, but he lifted his face and murmured, "With me." Suddenly he exclaimed, "Lavi! Where is Lavi?"

Koji helped him fumble with the collar of his tunic, and a brilliant yahavim burst into the air, zinging around in a joyous dance. Prissie squinted hard and gasped in recognition and lifted her hand, "Hi, you." She beckoned to the manna-maker who'd accompanied her down to the Deep. "You're looking much better."

The tiny angel with his puff of soft green hair lit on her fingers and twirled on the tips of his toes. Lavi's attention quickly returned to Ephron, though, for Koji was helping the injured angel rearrange his limbs. The rescued Observer's pants were badly torn, the cloth unraveling in the absences of seams, which left much of his legs bare. Prissie realized with a jolt that the mottling on his skin was probably bruising, and she couldn't begin to count the cuts, which were in various stages of healing. Her lips trembled, but her jaw came up. There had to be something she could *do*.

Although an angel's raiment could resist spot and wrinkle, Ephron was in desperate need of a bath. Dirt and dust gave his skin a slightly gray cast, with pale streaks to show the tracks his tears had followed. Prissie would have liked to take him down the hall to the bathroom, but that probably wouldn't work. No power. No lights. "Koji?" she whispered urgently. "How do angels wash themselves?"

"With water."

She bit her lip to keep back a sharp answer.

Koji's dark eyes took on a shine. "That is a good idea."

"Prissie?" She turned to find Beau holding out a basin of water. Her brother explained, "This other guy said you need this."

Lavi fluttered in a slow circle around Beau's head, then landed on the wide brim of what looked to be a heavy stone bowl. Her brother showed no sign of noticing the bright pixie testing the water with his toes. Prissie asked, "How many angels do you see?"

"Is that a trick question?"

She slowly shook her head and pointed to each, pausing to see his reaction. "Milo. Padgett. Koji."

Beau's eyes widened. "Koji's here? Wait. Koji's an *angel*?"

She stood awkwardly. "I ... um ... I guess I shouldn't have said anything."

"It's all right," Padgett said distractedly. "You may take your brother into your confidence."

"Then *yes*. Koji's an angel too."

"Figures." Beau gestured to Padgett and Milo. "But as far as I can tell, the only ones here are you, me, and them."

The worst of the mailman's wounds had been cared for, and the Caretaker had maneuvered Milo onto the floor so he could put away his wings for him. With deft motions, Padgett traced his fingers along the Messenger's shoulders and back, coaxing the billowing blue light into the unique pattern that contained an angel's furled wings. Finishing one side, he glanced up. "Take the basin, Prissie. And be careful. It's heavy."

She obeyed, taking the bowl that seemed to be filled with liquid light; it steamed lightly and smelled spicy. Arching his brows, Beau asked, "How many angels do *you* see, Sis?"

"Five. But there's probably more."

"And how long have you been seeing angels?"

Prissie hugged the basin to her chest and managed a weak smile for Lavi. "For a while. It's a long story."

"Tell me later?"

She nodded, and Beau returned to Milo's side. His wings were almost completely furled now, so the blue light was fading, but a second basin of water sat beside Padgett, a match for her own. Their warm glow was more than enough to see by.

Walking slowly so she wouldn't slosh the precious liquid, Prissie returned to Koji's side. He beckoned for her to join him on the floor. "You will support Ephron. I will wash him."

"How?"

The young Observer took charge. Pushing aside some of the clutter on the floor, he laid out her blanket. "Sit here, against the wall. You will support him the same way Taweel held Tamaes when he was injured. Remember?"

She nodded and took her place. With a little scooting and shuffling, Ephron lay limply in the circle of her arms, his head resting on her shoulder. For so long, he'd been nothing more than a name that put shadows in the eyes of her friends. Now, he was a solid someone whose suffering was all the more real in its aftermath.

When Koji straightened Ephron's legs, the injured Observer whined softly.

"I am sorry," Koji whispered.

Prissie was sorry too, but she couldn't say the words. Tears that she'd been holding back for what felt like forever blurred her vision. She wished for wings so she could wrap them around this angel and ease his pain. Wasn't she partially to blame for Ephron's prolonged captivity? If she'd prayed sooner, would he have been spared weeks or even months of torture?

Uneven tufts of flaxen hair brushed Prissie's cheek as Ephron shook his head. "Do not apologize. I am grateful." Fragile-looking hands found the arms locked around his chest, and he hung onto her. "More than I can express."

Koji took the folded cloth resting in the warm water, and pressed it to Ephron's cheek. "Should I remove the bandages?"

"Carefully," Padgett replied from across the room. "I'll be with you shortly."

As the strips of raiment binding Ephron's eyes fell away, Koji noticed Prissie's confusion and softly explained, "Ephron is blind."

Prissie closed her eyes, not wanting to see what lay beneath the bandages. Sick at heart. Sick to her stomach. She hid her face in the disarray of Ephron's hair and tried to focus on the scent of spices that perfumed the water. It occurred to her that if the basin was warm enough to steam in a room now exposed to the elements, she should have been freezing.

After some thought, she realized that while she was aware that it was cold, she wasn't uncomfortable. This was probably how it was for angels, and she was grateful that Padgett had extended their unique senses to her. Otherwise, her teeth would have been chattering by now.

A soft *whirr* of wings brought her out of her thoughts, and she looked up, expecting to see Lavi. But Omri stood on her shoulder; his small hands patted affectionately at her cheeks, brushing away the traces of her own tears. "If you're here, Taweel must be close."

"On the roof," Koji confirmed. Glancing up, he announced, "Jedrick is here."

Heavy footfalls sounded overhead, and Prissie looked up in time to see Jedrick toss aside some loose boards and shingles in order to widen one of the gaps. The Flight captain dropped into the room, bringing a wash of green light as his wings draped loosely behind him. Crouching beside Ephron, he said, "Here you are."

Lifting his face, the Observer answered, "I am here."

Jedrick's hand dropped to Ephron's shoulder. "Your name is still under my hand."

"I know it."

"I wish I could have protected you from all you suffered," the cherubim confessed. "Forgive me?"

"There is nothing to forgive, Captain. I am grateful to be under your wing once more."

"Amen and amen."

The matter was dealt with so simply. A straightforward apology. Immediate forgiveness. Prissie wasn't sure she could have done the same if, for instance, Margery were to say the whole Elise thing was a big mistake. *Could* people go back? Ephron certainly couldn't. He was blind. Unless the Caretakers were able to fix that for him. Weren't they capable of miracles?

"May I take your place?"

Prissie blinked up at Jedrick, then loosened her hold on Ephron. "Please do. Your wings will work better than mine."

The tall warrior blinked back. "Prissie Pomeroy, humans do not have wings."

Ephron actually smiled. "Have you no imagination, Captain? Many have wished for wings, but few for such noble reasons."

Jedrick lifted away the Observer as if he weighed no more than a feather, practically cocooning him in the folds of his wings. Prissie stood and brushed off her skirt as Padgett joined them. Koji wrung out his cloth and draped it on the edge of their basin, then stood beside her. His fingers brushed the back of her hand, and she caught at it, grateful to still have someone to hold onto.

"Sis?" Beau sat against the wall on the other side of the room, his eyes wide and his hair wild. Milo reclined against him in much the same way she'd been holding Ephron, and it looked as if her brother was holding on for dear life. "You're not talking to yourself," he said, the lift of his brows making the statement a question.

"No. Two more angels just came in," she reported.

Just then, a shaky hand lifted, covering Beau's. "There's nothing to fear," the Messenger murmured. "Or did I cover that part already? I'm a little foggy on the details."

"Milo!" Beau's arms tightened, and tears splashed down his cheeks. When he found his voice, he said, "If Zeke ever finds out you can fly, he'll never give you a moment's rest."

Their mailman's low chuckle was reassuringly familiar. "Some things are best kept secret."

"Yeah. I can do that much." Beau's face creased with concern. "Wish I could do more."

Milo's gaze drifted from Prissie to Koji, then back to Beau. "Given the circumstances, I think it's safe to assume there will be more."

Threshold Series

The Blue Door

Christa Kinde

ZonderKidz launches an exciting supernatural series for kids 11 and up. *The Blue Door*, the first book in The Threshold Series, introduces Prissie Pomeroy, a teen who discovers she can see what others cannot: angels all around. Even more startling is the surprising secret she uncovers about people she thought she knew. As she wrestles with this unexpected ability she must come to grips with the spiritual battles surrounding her. Especially when she learns she received this gift because God has a unique role for her in his bigger plan. But if she's to fulfill it, she'll need faith like never before. This exciting debut by author Christa Kinde draws on the rapidly growing interest in angel stories, an emerging trend in teen and preteen supernatural novels. Boys and girls alike will appreciate her gifted storytelling that captures their imagination with things beyond human sight. And parents will appreciate the family-friendly tone and godly messages maintained throughout this intriguing tale of adventure and spiritual warfare.

Available in stores and online!

Threshold Series

Angels All Around

(Threshold Series Prequel)

Christa Kinde

The prequel to the popular Threshold Series by Christa Kinde, *Angels All Around* is an illustrated short story set in a small town where not everyone is what they seem.

Amidst the chaos and confusion, will a new divine Messenger become one little girl's prince, and a fledgling Guardian become their knight, or will evil take its hold?

Includes a bonus first chapter from Book #1 in the Threshold series, *The Blue Door*!

ROUGH & TUMBLE

While you're waiting for *The Garden Gate*, you can read more about angels and the Pomeroy family on Christa's website, ChristaKinde.com. ***Rough and Tumble*** is an adventurous continuation to the Threshold Series, about a young angel named Ethan, who's sent to serve with the other Guardians of the Hedge surrounding the Pomeroy family farm. One mischievous little boy is about to turn Ethan's life upside down!

At just one hundred words, chapters are small enough to read on the fly—with daily updates and new installments.

Become a subscriber at ChristaKinde.com!

We want to hear from you. Please send your comments about this book to us in care of zreview@zondervan.com. Thank you.